Capitalist Sorcery

Capitalist Sorcery

Breaking the Spell

Philippe Pignarre
Paris, France

and

Isabelle Stengers
Université Libre de Bruxelles, Belgium

Translated and edited by Andrew Goffey

palgrave
macmillan

English translation first published 2011 by
PALGRAVE MACMILLAN

Palgrave Macmillan in the UK is an imprint of Macmillan Publishers Limited, registered in England, company number 785998, of Houndmills, Basingstoke, Hampshire RG21 6XS.

Palgrave Macmillan in the US is a division of St Martin's Press LLC, 175 Fifth Avenue, New York, NY 10010.

Palgrave Macmillan is the global academic imprint of the above companies and has companies and representatives throughout the world.

Palgrave® and Macmillan® are registered trademarks in the United States, the United Kingdom, Europe and other countries.

ISBN 978–0–230–23762–9 hardback

This book is printed on paper suitable for recycling and made from fully managed and sustained forest sources. Logging, pulping and manufacturing processes are expected to conform to the environmental regulations of the country of origin.

A catalogue record for this book is available from the British Library.

A catalog record for this book is available from the Library of Congress.

10 9 8 7 6 5 4 3 2 1
20 19 18 17 16 15 14 13 12 11

Contents

Acknowledgements

The authors would like to thank those people who read and criticised the manuscript, especially Didier Gille, Didier Demorcy, Alexandra Minvielle, Daniel de Beer, but also Groupe Culture et Paix, which shot down a first attempt in flames and thus forced us to reflect better on the position that we were intervening from. Thanks also to everyone who participated in a day of critical reading as part of the activities of GECo (Groupe d'études constructivistes) at the Université de Bruxelles and more specifically to Didier Debaise, Jonathan Philippe, Nathalie Trussart and Benedikte Zitouni, who introduced the different parts of the book.

During the writing of this book, we met militants from Attac, the CGT, the CFDT, from Sud, from Act Up and from the organisers of the intermittents and the précaires, all of whom encouraged us in our effort. Thanks to them.

Introduction: On the Witch's Broomstick

Andrew Goffey

Capitalist Sorcery: Breaking the Spell was written by Philippe Pignarre and Isabelle Stengers in 2004, five years after the enormous protests that shook Seattle at the end of November 1999. Since the events of 1999 there have been a series of more or less visible, more or less violently repressed anti-capitalist protests across the world. And since Pignarre and Stengers wrote their book, the collapse of the global financial markets and the increasingly high media profile of climate change have given added piquancy to any reflections about the problem of 'inheriting from Seattle'.

Pignarre, a writer, publisher and activist with nearly two decades' experience working in the pharmaceutical industry, and Stengers, a philosopher and historian of science, writer and activist most well-known, perhaps, for her collaborative work with Ilya Prigogine, might not strike the average political activist as the most likely pair to be writing about the problem of 'inheriting from Seattle'. However, on closer inspection, the bulk of Pignarre's writing, on psychotherapy and the pharmaceutical industry, the publishing house he set up (Les Empêcheurs de penser en rond), and the majority of Stengers's work display a concern (announced explicitly at the end of her *The Invention of Modern Science*) for exploring different aspects of the politics of knowledge(s), for generating new ways of bringing 'into politics' a range of issues that would not normally be considered in these terms. In fact, one of the first publications for Pignarre's house was a book by Stengers and Olivier Ralet about drugs and drugs policy in Holland that not only challenged prevailing 'psy' dogmas but also became a tool for 'users' wanting to meddle with what didn't concern them.[1] Even the recent essay by Stengers on Alfred North Whitehead (a figure whose philosophy most had probably consigned to the dustbin of intellectual history) displays a concern for 'the possible' that challenges the modern 'settlement', with its putting out of play of the domain of nature as an object of political concern.

But if one can thus discern a constant concern with political issues in their work, the reader might nonetheless experience a little perplexity at the authors' admission that not only were they not present in Seattle, but that the book they have written doesn't propose a historical account or any other kind of explanation of the event. In fact, it doesn't even try to offer a theory of anti-capitalist protest, which is what one might generally expect (even demand) from authors of scholarly historical and philosophical texts – especially if they write in French.

How Stengers and Pignarre came to be writing about the 'cry from Seattle', what they want to say about it and why they happen to be doing so together in terms of the notion of 'capitalist sorcery' are questions that are clearly answered in the course of the book, so it would be inappropriate to anticipate that discussion here. However, for the reader who is not familiar with their work – as well as the reader who is only familiar with their work in less obviously political areas – the claim that they make for the existence of a properly capitalist sorcery is one that can be usefully introduced and complemented by a discussion that draws on some of the other issues that this claim touches on. The specific problem of capitalist sorcery relates to issues that they tackle in their other writings. This introductory chapter thus seeks to gesture towards some of the crucial debates and discussions out of which the ideas that *Capitalist Sorcery* develops emerge.

How do you continue an event?

Capitalist Sorcery is neither an explanatory nor a theoretical text. What it tries to do is to think *with* the practices of some of the anti-capitalist protesters whose actions at Seattle gave a broader resonance to the cry 'another world is possible'. Events, whether they are assented to or disparaged from a distance (to say nothing of what happens to the immediate participants), raise the question of the difference that they make. This entails a decision – not necessarily a heroic decision, or one posed in the stark terms of an ultimatum (as when George W. Bush says 'you're either with us, or against us') – although there may be times when an event demands this kind of response. Rather, an event poses the question of *how* it might be linked to and continued:[2] is it in the mode of a sneering denunciation, as is seen so frequently in the media after demonstrations against globalisation? Is it in the mode of an activist question of how best to put to work energies that have been mobilised during a demonstration? Less direct ways of situating oneself in relation to it, generating other kinds of connection, are equally possible. One can imagine Seattle generating a psycho-social inquest, for example (why do all these people want to get out on the street and complain about the fruits of global capitalism?), or – more likely – high level boardroom re-visiting of investment strategies. Most frequently, though, one just expects a resigned shrugging of the shoulders: so what!

The authors do not have a general solution to this problem, partly because every event, when treated as such, *poses a problem*. It is the way that it does this, creating the potential for hesitation, that makes it an event. The approach that Pignarre and Stengers adopt here – affirming that, as Europeans with historical connections to a different kind of militancy, there is something to be learned with regard to Seattle – demands a curious mixture of very concrete, practical and highly speculative considerations. Their suggestion is that in the cry 'another world is possible', we need to take the opening which that possibility presents very seriously. For another world to be possible, *really* possible, the reality of that possibility effectively implies that we don't know quite how to respond, how to continue, how to inherit. Of course, we can always choose to ignore the event, but this comes at the risk of what might be called our damnation.[3]

That last paragraph sounds quite metaphysical. It is, but in truth this question of how to respond, in the face of expert judgement, for example, that denies the existence of an event (there's nothing to be seen here, move on please), is an issue that in some ways has preoccupied Pignarre and Stengers throughout their work, albeit in very different ways. It could be argued, for example, that the kinds of dissipative processes explored by Stengers's collaborator, Nobel prize-winning physicist Ilya Prigogine, pose precisely this kind of problem for the Newtonian world of the reversible laws of physics, wherein the arrow of time, the directionality of time, is merely phenomenal illusion. For the physicist, this raises the question of the extent to which our understanding of such processes can merely be attributed to calculative approximations. Can they? Or do they require the physicist to rethink his or her relationship to the physics s/he has inherited?

The example of the physics of irreversible processes – or indeed the invention of modern sciences more generally – might give the impression that the question of how one takes an event into account is a conceptual issue. It is, at least in the rather broad sense that events require thought, but it is also – and inseparably – a very practical, concrete, experiential matter. This is as much the case in science – which our epistemological proclivities generally lead us to imagine in purely theoretical terms – as it is more obviously so in the field of political struggles. The long history of alliances between science, state and industry has given the sciences a reasonably stable organization, which makes the prolongation of the possibilities that an event opens up a (relatively) routinised matter (notwithstanding the often violent nature of the debates such episodes can create). There are specific, if variable, *constraints* in scientific practice that shape the way in which events matter to it – constraints that help account for the enormously inventive nature of scientific practice.[4] But this is not the case for politics – or at least, not for the politics that matters. Politicians within the parliamentary-democratic system (or its near equivalents) are entirely caught up in a logic of killing politics that Pignarre and Stengers associate with capitalism. It is a logic that aims to 'naturalise' – and hence automate and de-politicise – political decisions. For the politics that matters, the same kind of enabling constraints as are evident in the experimental sciences do not exist,[5] and the question of continuing an event can become a really pressing – even life or death – matter. Schisms, depression, suicide – these are not uncommon occurrences in the field of political struggle, any more than are harassment, humiliation or just straightforward violence.

In *Capitalist Sorcery*, the speculative discussion takes a back seat to the more practical matter of the ways in which the practical possibilities that an event opens up are at constant risk of being poisoned, of turning bad. This issue – for which Pignarre and Stengers assume the figure of sounders of the depths – is one that is posed with particular acuteness when one asks the question of what and how anti-capitalist protesters can contribute to struggles in other domains. What relation can activists forge with other practices where the 'up front' question of opposition to capitalism has not necessarily been posed (and where, as a consequence, an anti-capitalist protester might not be inclined to see anything of interest going on *unless* it can be translated into the general terms of opposition to capitalism)? What are the risks of a militant conception of purity and fidelity to a founding event?[6] Pignarre and Stengers choose to address this issue by means of a pragmatic re-reading of Marx. Pragmatics is a term that the heritage of critical philosophy habitually associates with a politics of the expedient and the useful and the 'prevailing business culture'. However, throughout her work, Stengers has developed a detailed exploration of and experimentation with a rigorous re-formulation of pragmatics, specifically in relation to scientific practice, which contests this rather lazy reading. Here, as the discussion of what they mean by their pragmatic approach to Marx makes clear, it is the thoroughly modern position that Marx takes up vis-à-vis knowledge, the relationship between science and ideology, and the narrative pull of progress in his writings that calls for reformulation.

Marx, magic and modernity

Debates about the nature of modernity, something of an academic speciality over the last twenty years or so, might appear somewhat removed from the practical concerns evinced in *Capitalist Sorcery*. However, whilst Pignarre and Stengers do not want to formulate their concerns in terms of some more or less neutral, more or less abstract conception of rationality (as in Weberian disenchantment, for example), the question of modernity does have significant purchase on the issues that Pignarre and Stengers explore.[7] It is, we might argue, in the way in which Western societies habitually choose to characterise themselves that we can find the most perduring means for sorting between what is progressive – and therefore desirable – and what is backwards-looking, archaic, traditional – and therefore undesirable. And it is equally in this 'sorting' operation (from which militant politics has not been immune) that we find exposed what Pignarre and Stengers characterise as our 'vulnerability' to capture by capitalism.

For Marx himself there is something decidedly maleficent about capitalism, with the bourgeoisie as 'the sorcerer, who is no longer able to control the powers of the nether world whom he has called up by his spells'.[8] Quite aside from his specific references to Goethe and to the 'magic and necromancy' of commodities, Marx's understanding of capitalism has, as Marshall Berman has pointed out, a Faustian air about it. This air is nowhere more evident, perhaps, than in the *Communist Manifesto*,[9] wherein the drama of the bourgeoisie, sacrificed on the altar of the very development they initiate, is captured so lyrically. The tragic cast of the Faustian narrative taps into the thoroughly problematic link of the modern development of knowledge with the necessity of destruction, a process that Marx and Engels later characterise in the unforgettable passage 'all that is solid melts into air ...' Pignarre and Stengers comment at length on this passage in the *Manifesto* and the risks to which it exposes Marx: sober senses, not dreams! The ostensibly Faustian pact of modernity, the 'tragedy of development' as Berman puts it, finds resonances among both apologists – the Schumpeterians, with their praise of 'creative destruction' – and resolute militants – a figure like Alain Badiou, for example, with his reference to the 'ontological virtue of capital'.[10]

Where not associated with the movement of history, the broad characterisation of the risks of knowledge in terms of a sorcerous pact with Mephistopheles tends to yield a censorious recall to finitude, to the 'constitutive' limits that being human imposes on what we can know, and the concomitant reminder that science shouldn't overstep the mark. But if denunciations of science readily draw on the Faust myth, such denunciations are a bit like denunciations of capitalism: they rely on big concepts that are 'like hollow teeth'[11] and obviate the need for looking in more detail at what is going on. What gets forgotten, or ignored, when things are envisaged in terms of science or technoscience is that what Pignarre and Stengers call the 'mobilisation' of science is presumed – science could not act in the way it does without such mobilisation – but not understood. *How* scientists get mobilised thus becomes a crucial question.

The mobilised scientist, for Pignarre and Stengers, is a scientist whose practice has rendered him or her vulnerable to being pressed into the service of the construction of 'infernal alternatives'. That is to say, a scientist whose professional certainties about what are the right questions to ask can lead him or her to adopt a frighteningly dismissive stance with regard to anything that falls outside this position. The mobilised scientist stridently defends the position of science as the 'goose that lays the golden eggs' and his fearless certainties (outside the laboratory, at least) result in what Alfred North Whitehead, an early critic of the twentieth-century professionalisation and specialisation of knowledge, would call 'dogmatic denial': an enormous difficulty in dealing with what is external to science except in the derealising terms of 'beliefs', 'mere opinion' or 'illusions'. The mobilised scientist is a figure in search of a truth that would transcend the particularities of cultures, of interests, of opinions, a truth that arms him or her (mostly him) with the means of judgement.[12] For Pignarre and Stengers it is crucial *not* to imagine that every scientist is a 'mobilised' scientist, whilst it is equally important to understand that every one is vulnerable to becoming so, to fearing and scorning the public, and (increasingly) showing not a little resentment that perhaps the public is not quite as grateful as it should be, that it doesn't appreciate the important role that the brains of humanity play.[13]

Meddling with what doesn't concern you

Central to the account that Pignarre and Stengers propose here is the idea that there is a need to bring into the domain of politics issues that tend to rely on the idea that the public doesn't (need to) think. The notion of 'meddling with what doesn't concern you' might be explored in terms of what, following Bruno Latour, they call 'political ecology'.[14] In any case, it is crucial for the claims that they make about capitalist sorcery to counter the denial of politics that often occurs when it is said that an issue is simply a matter 'for the experts'. Expert authority is something that *should* translate with difficulty outside of the sphere in which specialist judgements makes competent colleagues agree. The issue is not one of opposing every technical decision that gets made but rather one of understanding that the kind of destruction that occurs under the aegis of progress or modernity depends upon an environment of stabilised, routine practices. It is in such routine practices that the tentacular grip of what Pignarre and Stengers call 'infernal alternatives' are produced, through a kind of politics that is the denial of politics.

Pignarre's extensive writings on the pharmaceutical industry are particularly illustrative in this regard. It is easy to argue – the texts have proliferated in recent years – that pharmaceutical production and the massive growth in the consumption of medicine demonstrates the logic of capitalist production in a particularly acute form. And it can't be denied that the pharmaceutical industry has been the locus of increasingly nefarious practices in recent decades, some of which are discussed by Pignarre and Stengers here.[15] The brutal – and racist – logic of the way that the (American) pharmaceutical industry lobbied against the use of generic HIV medication in South Africa springs to mind as an obvious example. However, over the course of a series of books, Pignarre shows why focusing on the 'ironic' operation of large-scale social forces behind the backs of practices, agents, institutions, regulatory frameworks and so on, means one ignores the ultimately political way in which the pharmaceuticals 'market' is fabricated.[16] With regard to depression in particular, it is rather tempting to argue that it is a 'capitalist illness' – this is an inference that is easily made on the basis of some well-known facts: that there has been a massive growth in the consumption of anti-depressants; that pharmaceutical companies make billions in profit from these 'head meds'; and that depression is particularly prevalent amongst the unemployed.

Pignarre's response to this line of reasoning is not to deny the presence of the capitalist elephant in the room (that would be rather difficult), or to conclude that anti-depressants are almost literally an opium of the masses. But rather than make deductions – even dialectically informed ones – on the basis of the mode of production of anti-depressants, he chooses to look *more closely at what is going on in the pharmaceutical industry itself*. How are anti-depressants produced, marketed, prescribed and consumed, for example? What elements are involved in this process?

The logic of big concepts (Modernity! Progress! The pharmaceutical laboratory as an application of Science!), or what Pignarre calls the 'intolerant abstractions' that the industry itself promulgates (today's profit is tomorrow's research, for example) dictates that we habitually tend to take some of the claims of the pharmaceutical industry at face value (if only to set them off against other abstractions). The claim that rational medicine uses specific molecules to target specific maladies can, when applied to mental health, lead to critical judgements along the lines of how nasty and reductionist it is to think that depression can be reduced to the specific interactions of particular molecules. Psychoanalysts regularly claim that drugs treat the symptom not the cause – with the implication that the patient is thereby avoiding some deeper truth about him or herself by taking anti-depressants. However, Pignarre points out that the appeal to science is itself a bit of a smoke-screen. The basic motor of the process of drug development in the pharmaceutical industry – double-blind, placebo-controlled drug trials – is not a technical application of scientific knowledge about the causes of mental illness, but a process in which one tests new molecules that are ever so slightly different to previous successful drugs and hopes that they are better. Specificity – the lock and key approach to drug design – is a biological shibboleth,[17] and the kinds of statistical correlations that the pharmaceutical corporations produce tell us only that drugs *do* work but not *how* they work: statistical correlations are not causes.[18]

In relation to mental health, though, there is more. Among other things, Pignarre notes that concurrent with the development of drugs that often do work in the treatment of mental health problems (are people who feel better on them deluded, as the 'opium of the people' argument might imply?), there has been a process of redefinition of the illnesses on which drugs are said to act. Sometimes even the creation of new ones. Pignarre gives the example of the development of 'male depressive syndrome', invented as a way to provide a diagnostic 'niche' for particular fenfluramine derivatives: the drug precedes the illness. The net consequence is, as he puts it, that the pharmaceutical machine 'on one hand invents the tools that allows the effects that it produces to be measured on the other'.

Pignarre's research into the pharmaceutical industry is illustrative of what it might mean to get a more precise understanding of what is going on in an area of the 'knowledge economy'. Getting a hold on the pharmaceutical industry here does not mean unveiling the truth about capitalist depression – that would be the gesture of ideology critique – but it does mean putting oneself in a position to understand the precise mechanisms by which a 'market' is constituted and a 'machine' operates, and how the kind of blackmail that the industry adopts (let us charge higher prices for these drugs or the research process will suffer) can be called into question. It is worth noting in passing that the involvement of groups like ACT UP in the question of the development of HIV medication entailed more than just militating for extra money to be spent on AIDS-related drug research. The latter ceases to be an effective strategy by itself once the specific 'mechanisms' of drug development are taken into account. The links developed by activists with biostatisticians at the National Institute of Health in the US and the advocacy of 'real-world messiness' versus what had been seen as the purity of science were important factors in effecting change and in the development of community-based drugs research initiatives for HIV.[19]

Frightening creatures

The problem with big concepts, which sanction the vision of pure science rather than hybrid, real-world messiness, is that they obviate the need to learn what it is that a particular situation requires. They capture thought in abstractions that yield no need – or desire – to pay too much attention to what is going on. As a consequence they make it difficult to get a hold on the operations that capitalism regularly accomplishes. Framing or justifying actions in terms of 'laws' – whether the 'laws of the market' or the 'laws of history' (and probably, in the future, the 'laws of thought'[20]) – results in processes of marginalisation, exclusion and destruction. Conceived along the lines of the 'laws of physics', such laws are imagined to hold 'whether we like it or not': recessions, unemployment, privatisation – so many unavoidable elements of 'harsh reality'.[21] From the practical point of view, that of how to act and the hold to be gained in a specific situation (in relation to, say, a particular restructuring operation), this particular version of realism simply precludes what Pignarre and Stengers would call the art of 'paying attention'. It is such an art that perhaps informs their preference for talking about the 'ethology of capitalism'.

The reference to ethology points up a sense of needing to investigate how capitalism operates in specific circumstances, how it might learn a particular kind of behaviour (for it is particularly responsive to threats of attack, and the violent reprisals of the state are only the most visible aspect of a considerably more ruseful and cunning system). The animal most appropriate to twenty-first-century corporate governance is not Behemoth or Leviathan but the octopus.[22] For Stengers, the fact that the octopus has a rather decentralised nervous system tallies with the idea that there is no central command post, no international conspiracy of the elites in charge of the global economic system (Swift's confederacy of dunces, at best). But the more general point is not just that an octopus is a tricky beast (the most intelligent of the invertebrates, according to some). It is that ethologists are learning that in order to get a better grip on what a particular living creature is capable of, one has to recognise that (unlike say electrons or earthquakes) living creatures are not indifferent to the questions that we ask of them.[23]

However, reference to an 'ethology of capitalism' might be a little too much for some. Isn't it a bad case of zoomorphism? In any case, what can octopuses tell us about the economic decisions of large corporations, or the conflicting priorities of different fractions of capital? Not very much is the simple answer. But the point here is not one of suggesting that political activists should become ethologists. Not in any obvious way, in any case.[24] Rather, the point is that if we think of capitalism in ethological terms we may be surprised to learn about the rather subtle ways in which its operations are conducted. We like to imagine the process of domestication – wild animals, the colonies, the economy – in terms of a logic of mastery, a logic that says we must submit to nature the better to master it. But ethology might just teach us to be a little more careful in this regard, because the 'nature' with which one is dealing has a subtle habit of responding to our questions in unforeseen ways. To be sure, the perpetual restructuring of work can always be explained by reference to critical shifts in the mode of production or strategies of accumulation. But the pragmatic value of doing so is less certain – there is always the risk (Pignarre and Stengers refer to it as one of 'poisoning') that the 'objective' judgements one feels licensed to make leave those they concern prisoners of an abstraction that makes it difficult for them to get a hold. How does a critique of the alienation of workers looking for a cure for AIDS enable these researchers to rethink the structure of the research process? Ethology requires us to focus a little more closely on the relationship that is established between the animal and the ethologist, a focus that, transposed to the field of politics should lead to a more nuanced understanding of the way in which capitalism constantly reorganises itself to prevent people getting a hold. The vampire squids of capitalism engage in the creation of 'infernal alternatives'.

The destruction of witches

Very little has been said in this introduction about witchcraft. Ignoring witchcraft would have been rather easy. Historical amnesia means that taking a distance from its claims to our attention is not difficult. Doing so here would also have made it possible, for example, to create two

Isabelle Stengers – the good one, who writes about science and the politics of knowledge – and the bad, slightly crazy one, who seemed to have got a bit new age-y and dreamed up some nonsense about witches. That would be a serious mistake though, because in the first place taking witches seriously is an intrinsic part of the effect that the authors want us to feel. Stepping out of the comfort zone of modern critical judgement, in which we sort between the good (reasonable, objective, progressive) and the bad (irrational, subjective, backwards-looking) without having to think about it too much *should* feel a little disarming. In the second place, a crucial point that Pignarre and Stengers make is that the abstract conception that we have of modern rationality – with all its destructive effects – only holds sway by the way in which it manages not to deal with things it doesn't understand and to close off the possibilities they open up. As Stengers puts it in her essay *The Science Wars* 'the favourite vice of our tradition [is] to construct a perfectly convincing argument that, as if by chance, has the capacity to dissimulate or condemn a question that it doesn't feel very certain about'.[25]

The simple historical fact of the matter is that witches were marginalised, excluded, persecuted and destroyed throughout Western Europe in the sixteenth century. Historical opinion as to why this took place is varied – some historians see it as intrinsically bound up with an emergence from the backwardness of the Middle Ages; for example, Sir Keith Thomas's influential account *Religion and the Decline of Magic* considers beliefs in the supernatural as inevitable for as long as more effective techniques for dealing with anxiety are not available. In *The Death of Nature,* Carolyn Merchant links the persecution of witches to a more general assault on a feminine-gendered nature. More recent work – such as that of Silvia Federici – has argued that the process of persecuting witches is an intrinsic element of the (recurrent) processes of primitive accumulation essential to the development of capitalism as an economic system.[26]

However, it is at the point that the link can be made between the persecution of witches and the emergence of capitalism that we need to be a little careful, so as not to misunderstand the point that Pignarre and Stengers want to make. When they say that they are seeking to take a lesson from neo-pagan witches such as Starhawk, and the practices they have developed, the historical fact of the destruction of witches is not their direct concern. Nor are they trying to suggest that these neo-pagans have developed some sort of hermeneutically privileged access to the past. Quite the contrary, in fact: it is the very factitious nature of the practices that these witches develop that most attracts their attention, as it communicates with what Stengers describes as the 'unknowns' of modernity.

It is in the context of her encounter with the work of ethnopsychiatrist, Tobie Nathan, that this question of the 'unknowns of modernity' acquires its most pressing importance for Stengers. For Nathan, working in the northern suburbs of Paris, the 'banlieues' that achieved notoriety in recent years for a spate of large-scale disturbances, the issue is one of how to respond therapeutically to immigrants – from a range of different ethnic groups across Africa – in an appropriate way. Can one take seriously the person who says that he or she has been attacked by a sorcerer? Yes, is the answer of both Nathan and of Stengers, but it is on condition that one understands that modern therapeutic practices – specifically psychoanalysis – must be vigorously contested over their pretension to speak in the name of the universality of 'the unconscious'. Psychoanalysis, Stengers argues, fails to understand what it does as a practice when it purports to explain the cure through quasi-scientific notions like 'transference'. The situation is very similar for her in regard to its treatment of hypnosis, with which Freud had quite serious difficulties.[27] Likewise, when Lévi-Strauss appeals to a notion of 'symbolic efficacy' as a way of explaining 'scientifically' how therapeutic practices work in 'other cultures',[28] there is a presumption to universality that entails not quite taking the claims of those cultures seriously. Following Nathan, Stengers argues that one must see therapeutic practitioners in non-modern cultures as 'technicians of the cure', a point of view designed to undercut attempts to explain the way that such practices work via the universality presumed by analysis.[29]

One very interesting consequence of the argument that Stengers develops with regard to non-modern therapies is that of the more general necessity of understanding technique without tacitly presupposing its hierarchical subordination to science.[30] And this point brings us back to witches again, for a technique or set of techniques that is not explained by science is, from a modern point of view, nothing but an artefact. However, considered from the point of view of the refusal to privilege *episteme* over *techne*, not only is artefactuality not necessarily a criticism, but the idea that there is something to be learned from the neo-pagans becomes a more credible claim – because a central element of what would otherwise allow what they do to be explained (away) is removed.

Pignarre and Stengers consider that the techniques of non-violent protest and ritual used by witches may be understood as an efficacious[31] form of 'existential catalysis', a notion that they borrow from Félix

Guattari. As Stengers puts it, 'to take the efficacy of a technique seriously imposes the need to understand it as being addressed to something more powerful than the technician'.[32] For the witches this is the immanent Goddess referred to by Starhawk in her writings. Guattari might have talked about it in terms of affect.[33] In any event, the process of existential catalysis concerns the production of an autonomous *power to become a cause for thought*,[34] that is to say, the cultivation of a sensibility and disposition to think and act.[35]

With the magic of this *power to cause*, Pignarre and Stengers bring witchcraft firmly back into the frame of the simultaneously speculative and practical concerns of their pragmatic approach to politics. Autonomy and the practical problem of being the initiator of a causal series are of course classical issues in the Western philosophical and political tradition.[36] What Pignarre and Stengers are getting at here is the idea that contrary to the professionally enhanced stupidity that arises when thinking gets stuck 'in grooves', as Whitehead put it, the artifices of witchcraft cultivate a power to 'activate' thinking. What Pignarre and Stengers find here is a practice that can teach us something about how to inherit from Seattle, without running aground on the rocks of those theories or critical judgements that would do our thinking for us. The bet that they make, when they mount the witch's broomstick, is that through the resonances that are introduced with the 'unknowns of modernity', force can be given to the insistent cry that 'another world is possible'.

Note on the translation

Pignarre and Stengers write in a remarkably precise way. That said, there are some textual issues that have meant adjustments to the structure of their writing have been necessary. First, written French is remarkably tolerant of long sentences, in a way that English isn't. Second, *Capitalist Sorcery* is a pragmatic, and somewhat circumstantial text, in the sense that it was written in large part to address a political problem that had immediate importance in France and Belgium. Thus some of the historical discussion, such as that dealing with 'mutuelles' in France, does not transpose directly into the Anglophone world (although there are some parallels of course). Third, the work for this translation was carried out for the most part in the second half of 2009, whereas the original essay was published in 2005, before the collapse of the banking sector or the serious incursions of climate change and the Gaia crisis (which Stengers explores in her more recent *Au temps des catastrophes*[37]). As a result some passages in the translation have been modified from the original French to reflect these changes. Professor Stengers's suggestions and advice were particularly helpful on this point.

A number of words posed certain kinds of problems in the translation. The French 'sorcellerie', for example, means indifferently 'sorcery' or 'witchcraft', and a sorcier or sorcière can be equivalently both a witch or a sorcerer or sorceress. Given the gender issues subtending the book as a whole though, it seemed appropriate to talk of capitalist *sorcery* and anti-capitalist *witchcraft*. In any case, the designations are not supposed to have a specific anthropological value – they are pragmatic, aiming at consequences. Another word that creates difficulties is 'prise'. This has a number of meanings in French – one talks of the 'prise de la Bastille' for example, to refer to the storming of the Bastille in 1789, equally it means 'hold', 'grip', 'capture', 'plug' or 'socket'. Here it has been rendered generically as 'hold', although the distinction has been made between the hold that capitalism has 'over' people and the hold that one can get 'on' it.[38]

It is almost certain that other words should have posed more of a problem than they actually did – and all the faults (and I hope there aren't many) in this text are mine.

* * *

I would like to thank Philippe Pignarre and Isabelle Stengers, both for writing their essay in the first place and for being so very helpful in the process of seeing this translation through to the end. I would also like to thank numerous other people for their suggestions, comments and encouragement at various stages – Brian Massumi, Erin Manning, Eric Alliez and Mick Halewood in particular. Thanks also to Priyanka Gibbons at Palgrave for her patience, and a special thanks to Paul Bains, who was instrumental in getting the project off the ground in the first place.

Notes

1. See Isabelle Stengers and Olivier Ralet, *Drogues. Le défi hollandais* (Paris: Les Empêcheurs de penser en rond, 1991). Stengers has also written a play re-imagining the relationship between Newton and Leibniz and a eulogy to Medea, from Greek mythology. More recently, Pignarre has explored the logic of activist political organization in a book on Olivier Besancenot and the French NPA (Nouveau Parti Anticapitaliste). See Philippe Pignarre, *Être anti-capitaliste aujourd'hui* (Paris: La Découverte, 2009); Isabelle Stengers,

Penser avec Whitehead (Paris: Seuil, 2002); Isabelle Stengers, *La guerre des sciences aura-t-elle lieu?* (Paris: Les Empêcheurs de penser en rond, 2001); Isabelle Stengers, *Souviens-toi que je suis Médée* (Paris: Les Empêcheurs de penser en rond, 1993).

2. The discussion here relates to Stengers's discussion in *Penser avec Whitehead* 'L'événement de son propre point de vue?' See Stengers, *Penser avec Whitehead*, pp. 212–28.
3. Damnation, a state that Pignarre and Stengers associate here with minions should not have any theological connotations. Deleuze (who, along with Guattari, is a constant reference for Pignarre and Stengers) suggests that damnation is a freely chosen state relating to a minimal capacity for being affected. See Gilles Deleuze, *The Fold: Leibniz and the Baroque* (London: Athlone, 1993). The distinction between possibility and probability is discussed in a number of places in Stengers's work. She draws a parallel with Deleuze's distinction between virtual and possible. See Stengers, *Penser avec Whitehead*, pp. 243–5.
4. On the complementary nature of the relationship between freedom and constraints in physics see Isabelle Stengers and Ilya Prigogine, *Entre le temps et l'éternité* (Paris: Fayard, 1988), p. 20.
5. In a footnote in 'Pour en finir avec la tolérance', Stengers remarks that politicians have been incapable of making the political problem constituted by the power of the economic imperatives to which they respond, exist. See, Stengers, 'Pour en finir avec la tolérance', *Cosmopolitiques II* (Paris: La Découverte, 2003), p. 340.
6. The allusion here is to Alain Badiou, of course. Much of what Pignarre and Stengers say here may be contrasted with Badiou's understanding of events and politics.
7. The question of modernity is incontestably at the centre of Stengers's concerns in her seven-volume series *Cosmopolitiques*.
8. A somewhat modified allusion to Goethe's poem 'The Sorcerer's Apprentice'. Karl Marx and Friedrich Engels, *The Communist Manifesto* (Harmondsworth: Penguin, 1967), p. 226.
9. Lukács makes the connection explicit. See György Lukács, *Goethe and his Age* (London: Merlin Press, 1968). As he points out, Marx himself refers to Faust in an essay from 1844. See Marshall Berman, *All That is Solid Melts into Air* (London: Verso, 1983).
10. See Alain Badiou, *Manifesto for Philosophy* (Buffalo, NY: SUNY, 1999), p. 57.
11. Gilles Deleuze and Claire Parnet, *Dialogues* (London: Athlone, 1987) p . 144. Translation slightly modified.
12. This sounds like a plea for cultural relativism. It is not. What Pignarre and Stengers mean is that a peremptory appeal to universality in certain kinds of knowledge practice means that those practices can *only* formulate their claims through exclusion or through taking short cuts that allow them to avoid finding out what a problem demands of them. This is exemplified in Freudian analysis, as we will see.
13. This is an issue Stengers tackles most directly in her recent *La vierge et le neutrino* (Paris: Les empêcheurs de penser en rond, 2006).
14. See Bruno Latour, *The Politics of Nature* (Cambridge, MA: Harvard University Press, 2004); Michel Callon, *Acting in an Uncertain World* (Cambridge, MA: MIT Press, 2009); and Andrew Barry, *Political Machines* (London: Athlone, 2001).

15. The extensive publications of David Healy provide detailed documentation.
16. See Philippe Pignarre, *Le grand secret de l'industrie pharmaceutique* (Paris: La Découverte, 2003).
17. See Jean-Jacques Kupiec and Pierre Sonigo, *Ni dieu ni gêne* (Paris: Seuil, 2003).
18. See on all this Philippe Pignarre, *Comment la dépression est devenue une épidémie* (Paris: La Découverte, 2001).
19. See, for example, Benjamin Shepard and Ronald Hayduk, *From ACT UP to the WTO: Urban Protest and Community Building in an Era of Globalisation* (London: Verso, 2002) and Bruce Nussbaum, *Good Intentions: How Big Business and the Medical Establishment are Corrupting the Fight against AIDS* (New York: Atlantic Monthly Press, 1990) and more particularly Steven Epstein, *Impure Science: AIDS, Activism, and the Politics of Knowledge* (Berkeley, CA: University of California Press, 1996).
20. As in a cognitivist/computational reworking of Boole.
21. Nietzsche once pointed out the suspiciously moral aftertaste of reference to the idea of 'chemical laws'. See F. Nietzsche, *Writings from the Late Notebooks* (Cambridge: Cambridge University Press, 2003), p. 24.
22. Or, indeed, the vampire squid, as one commentator remarked of the American investment bank Goldman Sachs. See Isabelle Stengers, 'Pragmatiques et forces sociales', *Multitudes*, 23 (Winter 2005/6).
23. See for example Roger T. Hanlon and John B. Messenger, *Cephalopod Behaviour* (Cambridge: Cambridge University Press, 1998). The work of Vinciane Despret, particularly her recent book *Quand le loup mangera avec l'agneau* (Paris: Les Empêcheurs de penser en rond, 2002) offers a detailed analysis of the way in which certain ethologists have developed a close attention to the ways in which, as she puts it, 'animals have transformed us in order that we transform them'.
24. Although one might read Deleuze and Guattari in this light. See Gilles Deleuze and Félix Guattari, 'On the Refrain', in *A Thousand Plateaus* (Minneapolis: Minnesota University Press, 1987).
25. Isabelle Stengers, 'La guerre des sciences', in *Cosmopolitiques I* (Paris: La Découverte, 2003), p. 84.
26. Keith Thomas, *Religion and the Decline of Magic* (London: Weidenfeld and Nicolson, 1971); Carolyn Merchant, *The Death of Nature: Women, Ecology and the Scientific Revolution* (New York: Harper and Row, 1980); Silvia Federici, *Caliban and the Witch: Women, the Body and Primitive Accumulation* (New York: Autonomedia, 2004).
27. And in an essay from 2002, *L'hypnose entre magie et science* (Paris: Les Empêcheurs de penser en rond, 2002), p. 154, Stengers argues that Lacan's argument that analysis creates analysts is actually a good definition of a 'sorcery machine', because 'in effect, the sorcerer only knows how to fabricate sorcerers'.
28. The relevant essays by Lévi-Strauss are 'The Sorcerer and his Magic' and 'The Effectiveness of Symbols'. See Claude Lévi-Strauss, *Structural Anthropology I* (New York: Basic Books, 1974).
29. The feeling of discomfort that Pignarre and Stengers want their readers to feel when they talk about witches is analogous to the discomfort that would be felt by an analyst in Nathan's ethnopsychiatric clinic when confronted with the way in which Nathan and his colleagues take seriously the invisible

beings that their patients bring with them. See Stengers, 'Pour en finir avec la tolérance'.

30. It is noteworthy that researchers in other domains have recognized the importance of calling into question the tacit hierarchy between *episteme* and *techne* for issues of development and resistance to domination. The work of Stephen Marglin is useful in this regard. See Frédérique Apffel Marglin and Stephen A. Marglin (eds), *Dominating Knowledge: Development, Culture, and Resistance* (Oxford: Oxford University Press, 1990).
31. See the comments on efficacy in Isabelle Stengers, 'The Cosmopolitical Proposal', in Bruno Latour and Peter Weibel (eds), *Making Things Public* (Cambridge, MA: MIT Press, 2005), p. 1001.
32. See Stengers, *L'hypnose entre magie et science*, p. 136.
33. It is in terms of a logic of the 'too powerful for me' that Deleuze characterizes affect in his *Abécédaire* (Paris: Editions de Montparnasse, 2004).
34. In 'The Cosmopolitical Proposal' Stengers uses the term *actant* to explain what she understands by efficacy. This is a crucial term for Latour in his development of actor-network theory, and one whose chemical connotations were not lost on Greimas, the semiotician who developed it. There are plenty of isotopes in narrative semiotics. See Stengers 'The Cosmopolitcal Proposal', p. 1000.
35. This question of sensibility in its relation to politics is one that Jacques Rancière has explored in recent texts, albeit in a somewhat different manner. See, for example, Jacques Rancière, *The Politics of Aesthetics* (London: Continuum, 2006).
36. See Kant's second critique, for example.
37. Isabelle Stengers, *Au temps des catastrophes. Resister à la barbarie qui vient* (Paris: La Découverte, 2009).
38. It is a term that Deleuze and Guattari both use, as does Bruno Latour, who uses it to consider precisely the action of 'divinities' in Tobie Nathan's clinic. See Bruno Latour, *Petite réflexion sur le culte moderne des dieux faitiches* (Paris: Les Empêcheurs de penser en rond, 1996), pp. 91–2.

Part I
What Happened?

1
Inheriting from Seattle

We are amongst the many people who keep the memory of 30 November 1999, Seattle, as the day when we began to breath a little more easily. A cry was born in Seattle, and its take-up elsewhere, from demonstration to demonstration, has – in one blow – made the stupefying evidence of what pretended, and still pretends, to define the future, fall into the past.

Of course, for others, there are other dates and places that take pride of place. The Chiapas in Mexico, January 1994, or December 1995 in Paris, for example. But we are not writing a thesis on history. We wish only to present ourselves: for us, it was Seattle and the cry 'another world is possible' which cracked the leaden cloak of impotence which, with its slogans (which we knew to be mendacious, but this knowledge had seemed day by day to become more and more insignificant), had little by little installed itself.

It is worth recalling the memory of all those voices, learned, enthusiastic or resigned, who said in the years before Seattle, 'you can't turn back the clocks', who said that the 'liberalization' of the world was inscribed in history as inevitably as gravity in nature.

This book is addressed to all those who, like us, have seen a series of slogans become established with a self-evidence that seemed to impose itself with all the inexorability of a rising tide, little by little washing away everything many of us had thought ourselves naturally entitled to, like castles made of sand. In all keys, the same refrain: 'the party is over, we have to be pragmatic now, accept the hard reality'. Not even a transitory reality but the 'hard reality' finally accepted after an orgy of ideological dreams. We didn't even know that we had been at a party, and – besides having very little that was 'real' about it – the reality being proposed was not hard but obscene, a collection of stupid and nasty dogmatic slogans claiming for themselves the authority of pseudo-economic theories that at first made us laugh. We were wrong to have laughed.

'Another world is possible' is a cry. Its power is not that of a thesis or a programme, whose value would be judged by its plausibility. It doesn't authorise any kind of triumphant putting into perspective or offer any kind of guarantee. In any case, that is why the singular 'another world' is appropriate: it is not a matter of an allusion to a particular world that we would be able to define, nor is it of any matter what other world it is (any other world than this). It is a matter of appealing to the possible against the inexorable allure of the process that has set in and, of course, continues today more than ever. It is a matter of breaking something of a spellbinding order, a stunned impotence of which even those who were still struggling could sense the proximity. We say that this cry is the name of an event, and that the force of this event is the manner in which it makes this question exist for those who respond to it: how is one to inherit, to prolong, to become the child of this event?

Becoming the child of an event: not being born again into innocence, but daring to inhabit the possible as such, without the adult precautions that make threats of the type 'what will people say?', 'who will they take us for?' or 'and you think that is enough?' prevail. The event creates its own 'now' to which the question of a certain 'acting as if', which is proper to children when they make things (up), responds.

Of course this leaves the door wide open to a series of accusations, because this can be confused with a 'becoming irresponsible' or 'taking one's dreams for reality'. But that isn't very important, because we aren't addressing ourselves to adults, only to those who are also asking themselves how to respond to something that made us 'young again', which demands that we shake off the weight of the 'what's the points?', of one's doubts about the legitimacy of intervention, of the knowledges of the risks of misunderstanding. 'Acting as if' what the event makes one dare to do was what it demands, what creates its prolonging. And, inversely, not to act as if what we were writing was authorised by the slightest position of legitimacy. One is always somewhat overtaken by what one writes, but most frequently this remains a private experience. Becoming the child of an event is that too: not to present ourselves as spokespersons, prophets of the event, but as obliged by something that constrains us to abandon the precautions that befit authors.

It is, then, to the force of the event that this text testifies. We – Isabelle and Philippe – knew that one day or another we would write together, because our trajectories called out towards one another in ways that we wanted to explore. From our distant starting points – the philosophy of physics and revolutionary militant action – we had both followed paths that brought us into proximity. One of us asked what had happened to us such that that to which the sciences – when they are alive – testify (the capacity of researchers to work and to create together) is found so little elsewhere, whether in the so-called 'human' sciences or in political groups who nevertheless set out to create the means to resist and to open up the future? How – beyond clichés and slogans – is one to grasp the manner in which those who we define as the adversary to beat proceed, asked the other, whom the aleatory fortunes of political struggle had led to work in the pharmaceutical industry, where he was finally able to create a publishing structure which became worthy of its name through struggle: 'Les Empêcheurs de penser en rond' – those who hinder thinking in circles. For us both, what makes force? what makes weakness? had become the primary questions, before the true and the false, the just and the unjust.

And we both had the fortune to be nourished by practical experience, which this text will sometimes echo. Participating in groups experimenting with the situations and constraints that raise the possibility of thinking and inventing together allows one of us to approach the demands of an encounter between 'happiness and politics', because such a possibility is political. It is that without which politics is nothing but blind routine or sacrificial militancy, or both. To seek out and encourage authors who wish to avoid thinking in circles meant for the other to be on the lookout for minoritarian propositions, for the resources for thought that survive on the margins, creating opportunities for encounters and bringing into relation.[1]

So we knew that in one manner or another, we would have to produce together what we had learned, both of us together and each of us alone or with others. But it is the event – Seattle and its repercussions – that fabricated the 'we' that will prevail in this text. The question of how to inherit (from) Seattle has brought us together in a way that renders what comes from the one or the other indiscernible, because it has obliged us to risk an adventure that stirs up everything we have learned. And obliges us to risk a movement that makes us vulnerable. This vulnerability is the condition for addressing those who, like us, are engaged – and thus called into question – by the event.

Evidently there are many manners[2] of inheriting (from) Seattle. We knew which one we wanted to resist, the manner that called on us to 'behave like adults', the one that transforms the cry into a programme. We wish to be the inheritors of the heteroclite crowd that made Seattle such a surprise. Those who gathered there were multiple, and often conflicting, minorities. Perhaps what united them was, in a fleeting manner, a vision, but not at all a theory nor even a common definition of the society for whose sake they exposed themselves to blows from truncheons, tear gas and prison. Yet they did not go to Seattle, or to the other demonstrations that followed it, spontaneously. There was a whole labour behind it that we have largely ignored in Europe, partly because the American press was careful not to give it any coverage. But perhaps it is also because the American activist movements that have managed to survive and to proliferate, despite the Reagan years and what came after it, don't resemble our own militant groups and organisations very much.

At the end of this book we will be thinking with some words that don't translate very well into French – notably *reclaiming* and *empowerment*. This is part of the risk to which we have exposed ourselves: the bet is that something happened in the States from which we can learn. Not to be converted or to imitate, but to accept the test of a detour via something that most frequently seems only to merit a disdainful shrugging of shoulders – a strange idea for us, belonging to old Europe, the inheritor of rationalist scepticism.

It is not surprising that from social forums to organised movements one hears it said that it is necessary for 'constructive propositions', a 'social project' to follow on from the cry 'another world is possible'. There's no need for denunciation, for talking immediately of recuperation, of appropriation, of betrayal. We understand very well that faced with the problems of a world where things really are going very badly, there is an urgent need to organise a real opposition, with everything serious that that implies. And whoever says 'opposition' often says 'credible alternative': one has to display what one would do in the place of those who are in power today. But it is precisely this 'in place of', this interchangeability that makes us pause. It is at this point that we accept the accusation of irresponsibility that accompanies every 'becoming child'. It seems to us that offering other solutions without having grasped the means, without having created the means for posing the problems differently is to behave as if everything could be sorted out with a bit of good will or humanity. It underestimates the immense challenge that the urgent cry 'another world is possible' designates.

But there is another, antagonistic, version of the way in which the cry from Seattle can be inherited. Many of the groups who have become active, with whom we would wish to work and to learn, affirm that what they do is not politics, because politics is recuperation, placing under tutelage, betrayal. We are certainly amongst those for whom 'taking power' implies changing our relation to the power that it is a matter of taking, that is to say, changing the very definition of power itself. But in the disgust with politics as it is conducted, however justified it may be, there is sometimes a disgust with politics itself, its negotiations and compromises. Something like a will to purity, which doubles up with certain effects of terror, a passion for selecting between the good and the bad. We are very frightened of 'the pure', the defenders of a movement whose spontaneity, whose 'spirit', has to be protected from all calculation – because any calculation would be a mutilation, and from all preoccupation with power – because power, whatever form it might take, corrupts.

We aren't the only people to know this situation, of being trapped between two fires. But it is this situation to which we will give the power to make us think, imagine and be adventurous. Adventurous only with words, certainly, but we think that words have a power. They can poison, imprison in dilemmas, provoke endless disputes. They can also create, make exist or confirm possibilities weakened by the poison of other words. We will venture words that will, we hope, help in inhabiting the precarious possibility born in Seattle, a trembling possibility where previously probability reigned. Words that will help in inhabiting this possibility without crushing it, without taking it hostage, without conferring on it the power to designate its guardians, those to whom it would belong to mobilise the masses, or the citizens or even the multitude.

We will equally attempt to learn to separate ourselves from these other words, which fabricate such guardians. This signifies learning to separate ourselves from a certain past, in which mobilisation was an end in itself, and doing this without for all that proclaiming a decisive rupture from those who resisted, thought and struggled before. In short, we are attempting to *construct* a way of inheriting from Seattle and its multiple pasts, a way which is inhabited by the question of what the cry that made the event obliges us to.

We have been asked, and we have asked ourselves, who we take ourselves for. In what way does the life and experience with which we think allow us to play the kind of role we seem to pretend to? We are a little indifferent to questions of right, of legitimacy, but not the question of ways of doing. 'Do as if' is not in the slightest 'do no matter what'. Becoming children, children of the event, is not to babble on every note of the scale, it is an experiment that requires a certain discernment, a precise way of situating oneself so as to resist self-indulgence. The contrary of infantilism.

What type of sensibility to the event have our trajectories – respective and in common – given us? How is one to avoid the caricature of becoming-child, which consists in giving in to the temptation to 'take up all the space', all the places available? We hesitated a lot before realising that we would fail if we could be attributed the position of the person holding the map indicating the direction to take, the distance to cover, the useable paths and steps to follow. We do not know. We are neither prophets nor theorists. What makes us think are rather the modes of thought, the habits which might make what was born at Seattle run aground, a little like a boat runs aground, gets stuck in the mud.

We are not strategists, but we are not tacticians either, because one is only a tactician in the hand-to-hand combat of a particular situation. And if we have spoken of a boat, it is not only because the power of the event is that of putting those who respond to it in the same boat together – a more or less heteroclite crowd gathered with no other principle of selection. It is also because the image of the boat communicates with the possibility of a role that could guide and constrain us. In a long forgotten book, we effectively encountered, amongst the members of a ship's crew, the character that might work for us, that of the sounder of the depths.[3]

Sounders of the depths may well stay at the front of a ship, but they do not look into the distance. They cannot announce directions nor choose them. Their concern, their responsibility, the reason for the equipment they use is the rapids where one can be smashed to pieces, the rocks that one can hit, the sandbanks where one can run aground. Their knowledge stems from the experience of a past that tells of the danger of rivers, of their deceptive currents, of their seductive eddying. The question of urgency poses itself for the sounder of the depths as it does for everybody else, but his or her proper question is and has to be: 'can one pass through here, and how?' – whatever the urgency, whatever the 'we have to' or the direction chosen may be.

Sounders of the depths can be mistaken, but they know that the fact that they discern hazards accurately or not doesn't have the slightest importance if no one hears them. For them it is not a matter of being correct by themselves, or of waiting for the future to prove them right. It is this boat here that is their reason, this boat here which, in our case, gathers those who the cry 'another world is possible' has engaged, but who engage with languages that often divide them, with past histories that could destine them to sterile confrontations. Sounders of the depths should not invent words that are to be understood as beyond division, as if they were authorised by a transcendence in the presence of which everyone must kneel: that is the role of the prophet, or his substitute today, the theorist. The words to be created ought rather to serve as antidotes to what transforms divergences into oppositions, what makes us dream of a homogeneous unanimity, of a judgement that will at last confer on history the power to recognise those who had seen correctly.

Some people place their confidence in urgency, that of an Earth whose ravaging would force us to understand each other under pain of being destroyed. Others evoke opposition to a common enemy as sufficient to found the necessary understanding. We fear the confidence in the pedagogical power of catastrophes a great deal and the power given to the common enemy to unite us leaves us more than doubtful. That is why we feel ourselves bound to the position of 'sounders of the depths', attentive to the danger of the traps that menace us: that of thinking that tolerance with regard to divergences ought to be enough; that of thinking that we can take shortcuts with regard to the practices that may turn these divergences into a force. Linking divergences with practices, not with ideas, will be a way to exhibit the nightmarish character of what tolerance can always indulge in: the nostalgia or hope that makes of the difficulties we have in understanding each other that which we 'have to accept'… for the moment. It is the danger of this 'having to' that makes us write, imagine, affirm.

Throughout this text, we will employ an affirmative style. Make no mistake: it is not about 'evidence' that everyone ought to accept as going without saying. Rather, it is about propositions that attempt to transmit effectively – affectively – a feeling for the dangers just as much as the possibilities for us of protecting ourselves from them. Perhaps we should have been more prudent, littering our text with rhetorical questions, reminders that it is we who are speaking, not the truth. We have been unable to: each time it was as if we wanted to 'convince' a fictive, general auditorium, whereas we are addressing ourselves to those who, like us but in different ways, feel they have 'embarked'. 'As if' the event that obliges this text, which has made us embark, required the affirmation that exposes, not the prudence that reassures.

2
What Are We Dealing With?

The cry of Seattle went up against those who pretended to represent the only world possible. But who are they, where does their power come from, what does this power consist in? For some, the reply goes without saying. We are dealing with what Marx characterised as 'capitalism'. Let us say it plainly: we are amongst those who do not think that the heritage of Marx belongs to an outmoded past. And moreover we think that capitalism has in fact itself seen to the demonstration of the Marxist thesis according to which the problem with it is not simply a matter of a transitory disequilibrium, of an excess of power monopolised by the economy, that should 'naturally', 'logically', or 'progressively' correct itself. If, forty years ago, the perspective of a 'humanisation' of capitalism could still be credible for many, it is for us today a hypothesis that has been refuted.

But we say all that without the slightest triumphalism. In experiments that are carefully thought through and prepared in the laboratory, the refutation of a possibility can certainly be equivalent to the verification of a rival possibility. But when it is a question of human histories, this 'either/or' doesn't have much sense. The refutation of the possibility of progressive regulation that prevents the 'excesses of capitalism', that places it in the service of humans, is not equivalent to the verification of a rival possibility, the necessity of a passage through 'revolution'. All the less today now that we are dealing with a rather paradoxical situation: more than ever, what Marx called capitalism can certainly be considered as deploying all its effects, but there are many who will say to us: are you 'still' Marxist? Marx's oeuvre is disqualified whilst his diagnosis is verified.

We want to think 'with' this paradox, not against it, not to denounce the triumph of ideology, the blindness of those who have accepted what is often presented as a 'historical judgement': Marxism has been defeated. That doesn't mean that we want to think 'with' the rhetoricians of the end of history and other mediatico-academic order-words.[1] The challenge for us is to learn to coexist with those who do not accept that any fight must be subordinated to the strategic needs of the ultimate struggle against capitalism, defining as an end in itself their possible 'conversion' to Marx. Certainly we are tempted to 'explain' to them that capitalism condemns their hopes and prospects to being nothing but a hollow dream. But we want to give ourselves the means to learn from their determined pragmatism, and that requires that we ask ourselves what our explanations would bring to them, apart from an imperative to denounce: 'you must denounce capitalism, it is responsible for everything against which you are fighting'. Well, if capitalism were to be put in danger by denunciation, it would have collapsed a long time ago.[2]

We define ourselves as 'anti-capitalist' and in this sense as inheritors of Marx. But such a definition is more than insufficient: it is silent on what today has become (again) an open question. And it is not a matter of adding some sort of positive, constructive 'pro' to the 'anti'. We are rather indifferent to prefigurations of a reconciled or communist world if they do not communicate with the capacities of imagining, creating and resisting today. Our question is in appearance much more modest, because it bears on the 'how': how are we to attempt to 'deserve' that others – who define themselves differently or who refuse all definition – rejoice in our existence as we rejoice in theirs? The danger that obliges us to think as sounders of the depths would be to define the paradox that we are coming up against – Marx's oeuvre disqualified whilst his diagnosis is confirmed – as the effect of a simple misunderstanding with regard to this oeuvre, doubled by a blindness induced by media and academic propaganda.

We are addressing ourselves here to the inheritors of Marx. And we are doing so not 'amongst ourselves' but in the presence of those with whom it is now a matter of coexisting: those groups in struggle, who, like the feminists, refused the order of priorities proposed in the name of class struggle; like the radical ecologists, who have had to struggle against the assimilation of nature to a set of resources to be valorised; like the peasants, who have had enough of the taste of productivism; like the indigenous peoples who have to deal with the unanimous judgement that identified their practices with simple superstitions, etcetera.

We know that Marx cannot be confused with the Marxisms with which all the above have collided. We know that it is possible to defend him, sometimes also against himself, but also to refer to all those thinkers who have prolonged, complicated, enriched and modified Marx's theses. Besides, some are in our hearts and our thoughts. Michel Foucault, whose investigations forbid all naivety regarding the coexistence of capitalism with a 'good society', with its schools, hospitals, its permanent efforts to defend itself in a human manner against what menaces it, to rehabilitate deviants, care for the mad, etcetera. Gilles Deleuze and Félix Guattari, who responded to the challenge of thinking together capitalism and the constitution of modern states. We are indebted to them, we learned to think with them.

But as sounders of the depths, we also know that everything that looks like an argument from authority constitutes a fault. It is not by defending Marx that his heritage can be prolonged. It is not by complaining about misunderstanding, misreading, about the Marx innocent of the crimes he is accused of. As if rediscovering the 'true Marx' was what would create a new point of departure, acceptable to all. Those in whose presence we find ourselves had their own point of departure, often against Marxisms, and they will only be interested in what the inheritors of Marx can bring today when they talk of capitalism. In fact, an inheritor/descendant of Marx would have to admit the legitimacy of the test that we are proposing, that of admitting that the question of a 'good' reading of Marx is only primordial if this reading, disengaging him, for example, from Marxist interpretations, communicates with new possibilities of pertinent action.

The crucial point is not to reach agreement on what Marx wrote, but to prolong the question that he *created*, that of this capitalism whose hold it is a matter of combating. And to prolong this question, it must be remembered that what Marx called 'capitalism' has nothing to do with an empirical matter of fact, like earthquakes, for example, which allow for the separation of the observation of their occurrence and discussion as to the possibilities of confronting their catastrophic effects. Capitalism doesn't even have the 'identifiable' mode of existence that it has been possible to attribute to those regimes and movements that are called 'communist'.

Let us recall the *Black Book* that added up all the deaths 'caused' by communism.[3] This type of calculation is impossible with capitalism, because there are always other actors on stage who seem much more concrete. The coup d'état in Chile? Isn't accusing Pinochet, the Chilean army, the CIA, Kissinger enough? Danone closes a factory? One can criticise the directors of Danone, or – to hear them talking – the terrible necessities of international competition, or the selfish demands of shareholders. Why double all that up with the abstract accusation 'capitalism', in the service of which all these protagonists would be working?

Of course, certain people, in the United States above all, call themselves capitalists, but not in Marx's sense. They are not in the service of 'Kapital', as abstract power of redefining the world. If they honour something, sometimes with tears in their voices, it is 'the market' instead, whose power of arbitration – which may well be implacable, but is the sole power that is just – is the object of incantatory celebrations. Of course this 'market that decides' can be as tinkered with, bodged together and complicated as the French nation, in whose service so many died. But it must be said that the market, as much as the nation, has modes of existence to which the capitalism identified by Marx cannot pretend. Because no one – except the anti-capitalists and sometimes, during major crises, a few commentators, who are suddenly and temporarily disturbed – ever evokes capitalism as a 'cause'. Those who denounce it can therefore give the impression of being paranoid, seeing behind all those who actively pursue their own interests, their own strategy, a Grand Puppeteer pulling all the strings, but whose existence doesn't add an iota of intelligibility to the situation.

To inherit from Marx, it is therefore not enough to see in the situation today the confirmation of capitalist logic such as he diagnosed it. This diagnostic must be made to exist in an effective manner, one that makes a difference and doesn't confine itself to the redundancy of denunciation. And we take this requirement all the more seriously because, in other instances, we are very interested in the calling into question of 'big concepts'. For example, the manner in which Bruno Latour attacks notions of 'Society' or of 'Science' or of 'the Scientific Spirit', which serve to explain, whereas they are what should be explained.[4] Whereas one should follow, narrate, politicise the heterogeneous multiplicity of ways of doing, evaluating, co-ordinating, making 'non-humans' of all sorts intervene, with whom, thanks to whom and through whom, new manners of doing, evaluating, co-ordinating, become possible. For better and, often, for worse.

In fact, from our own experience, we have been able to measure the effect of 'grand explanations/explanatory schemas'. We have both of us on many occasions taken to task the reference to 'scientific method', which is liable to justify the unacceptable and the stupid, to lump together the most astonishing success and the most disabling bureaucracy of statistics and measurements. And we have also come up against 'social explanations' when, for instance, we have participated in the calling into question of drug policy, with its assimilation of the 'addict' to either a delinquent or sick person (refusing to seek help means to be a delinquent). Some impeccably progressive personalities objected at the time that it was a false problem, because drugs should be understood as a 'social problem': it was therefore necessary to talk about exclusion, unemployment – young drug addicts were firstly victims. That may well be the case but the consequence of this argument was to de-politicise the situation, because there was nothing to learn from and no link to forge with drug takers, suddenly plunged into general considerations, where they became 'like all the others': all victims.[5]

No more than we can see a triumph of science or of social lucidity in the possibility that youngsters in the banlieues might one day go around wearing t-shirts bearing the slogan 'I am a social problem', can we be satisfied with analyses that always come back to the same thing: it's capitalism's fault. The question is thus one of knowing what today one can 'gain' by putting capitalism centre-stage and calling it into question. That is to say, what it is that those who present themselves as anti-capitalist can specifically bring to militants from Greenpeace, for instance, or other associations in struggle? Tolerance, standing 'shoulder to shoulder', goodwill are not enough when a missionary desire to enlighten or to convert lurks or may be suspected of lurking behind them. And no protestation to the contrary is ever enough to allay the suspicion. The only thing that can succeed here is a manner of contributing that is proper to a particular situation, which may be evaluated as such and whose pertinence others can recognise.

But the question can equally be posed to others, to all those who proceed by 'grand explanatory schema'. It's the fault of Capitalism, Society, Technoscience, Patriarchy ... All these denunciations can certainly announce and inspire highly significant practices of resistance and struggle. We are not judges and what we write should never be understood in terms of 'here is what has to be done' or not done. From our point of view as sounders of the depths, what matters is the way in which such struggles will be able to protect themselves against what menaces them all. What they have in common is to invoke something that, if one doesn't look out, can very easily assume all the characteristics of a truth that transcends conflicts and explains them. As a result political practices – practices that are addressed to those issues that divide and create hesitation – are referred to a theatre of appearances, where one agitates, discourses and wrangles whilst the 'real stakes' are elsewhere. As if, consequently, politics was destined to disappear when what is really responsible for everything that divides us has finally been beaten.

The inheritors of Marx are thus not alone in this test, in what we will call the test of a *political creation* of questions that draw us together and divide us at the same time. The relevance of such a test is perhaps even the defining feature of this epoch, what makes us talk of the 'cry' from Seattle, calling for the possibility of another world without, however, being able to define the path that would lead there. We know today that, in the eventuality of a victory against the 'enemy' – however that enemy might be identified – those questions that are associated with politics will not vanish as if by magic. The world we would inherit would not be a world of plenty.

To have made political questions proliferate by tearing them away from the fields of expertise in which they were confined is the major contribution of political ecology. Endangered species, climate change, pollution, the sharing of water resources, the energy crisis, desertification, all of this is starting to enter into politics. Whatever the future, the struggle for these themes to remain political, for them not to be confiscated by supra-political agencies that would act in the name of a so-called consensual rationality and would become the true masters of the Earth and its inhabitants, is for us, primordial.

Here the danger can be made more specific. There is a most menacing proximity between the seductions of the denunciation of appearances and the expert pretence of defining what must produce agreement beyond the hesitations and conflicts that political practices attempt to address. When shared by those who work in the name of science, and those who denounce in the name of the truth, the contempt for politicians is a deadly pitfall.

Of course, to affirm that one must see to it that nothing transcends politics is a bit astonishing, because politics is also one of those questions that divide. It can figure neither as a final recourse nor as a promise, because it appears today as empty, disqualified. 'They're all the same', we hear. For many of those who suffer, everything of which they are the victims 'is the result of politics'. And that is where we must take on our responsibilities as 'sounders of the depths'. If those who think and become active in a struggle 'against capitalism' can 'bring something to the table' it will be necessary for them to find the means of transforming anti-capitalism – which all too frequently serves as an instrument of denunciation that makes all questions amount to the same thing – into a tool for deploying these questions politically.

Such then will be the manner in which we will try to present the specificity of what an anti-capitalist position can bring to the positions of other struggles. It is a matter of inheriting from Marx, who developed a critique of political economy, that is to say, of the way in which the economy was transformed into *a politics that kills politics*, that gives itself the authority of a rationality that demands unanimity. It is a matter of making capitalism exist as something the effects of which we testify to whenever we hold politics in contempt: something the very functioning of which kills politics.

3
Daring to be Pragmatic

We are inheritors of Marx in the sense that, for us, capitalism exists. Yet we have just characterised its mode of existence in a manner that many of his other inheritors would characterise as 'symptomatic'. Politics, according to many Marxist readings, is simply a translation of relations of force. On this count there is nothing to kill, only ectoplasm 'finally' dismissed to the kingdom of appearances to which it belongs. We do not want to pose the question of knowing if such an objection is authorised by Marx, or if it is the fruit of a 'false reading'. What is important, for us, is that the thesis by which it is authorised, the thesis that results in the disqualification of politics, is a poison. Whoever has been poisoned is doomed to define others as 'misguided', lacking the correct perspective, and not as a protagonist with whom it is a matter of learning to coexist politically.

However, the simple fact that we pose the question of the mode of existence of capitalism may seem rather arrogant. Do we know nothing of the intelligibility that the research of Marx and those who have inherited from him has produced in this regard? Aren't we turning our backs on an undertaking to elucidate that hasn't stopped exposing the traps of false transcendence, that has asked tirelessly 'how does it work?' Worse still, isn't linking the question of the mode of existence of capitalism with that of asking 'what can be brought to the table?', as we do, to give in to the pragmatic platitude that pretends to judge an idea by its *cash value*, by what it yields?

We are not going to enter here into disputations about text and about definitions. We prefer to say, from the word go, that *there is well and truly a pragmatism in Marx*, and that we desire very much to inherit and prolong it, whilst putting it to the test of what we are dealing with today. This has to be said[1] – not so as to scandalise but so as to be able to address ourselves to what would otherwise risk creating poisonous misunderstandings. We are thinking of all of those who, every day, find themselves opposed with a scornful 'stop thinking so much, be pragmatic!' And also of those who would see in this thesis the pretension to a discovery that would overturn every perspective in the history of thought.

To those who have learned to hate this word 'pragmatic', we will say: don't you feel that the injunction to 'be pragmatic' is an insult to the 'concerns', the *pragmata*, that you were trying to address? Don't leave this word in the mouth of your enemies! To the readers of Marx, we will say: do you not recognise that the definition that Marx brought to capitalism was inhabited by the question of action, that the categories that he associated with it communicated with the question of knowing what forces could resist it without allowing themselves to be either seduced or fooled? Not to 'interpret' but to transform doesn't signify that everything is good from the moment that it activates transformation, but that the truth of an idea or of a definition or of a hypothesis is nothing other than their verification, that is to say, the way in which they can produce consequences that orientate action.

And the 'pragmatic' definition of truth is precisely that. Pragmatism is an art of consequences, an art of 'paying attention' that is opposed to the philosophy of the omelette justifying the cracked eggs.[2] We don't want to say any more than this. Or any less, because it has an important consequence: we will never say that capitalism is 'pragmatic'. It is rather the anti-pragmatic system par excellence, because the systematic enterprise of re-definition associated with it is not obliged by any kind of verification at all, nor by a thinking concerned with consequences. Capitalism is what never stops inventing the means to submit what it deals with to its own requirements – and the consequences don't concern it at all: it externalises them (others can pay), or defines them as the potential matter for new operations.

To attempt to inherit a 'pragmatic' Marx is not to pretend to inherit the 'true Marx'. Nor is it a matter of an arbitrary reading. It is a pragmatic risk, to be evaluated by its consequences. And one of these consequences is that the imperative stated by Marx – do not interpret but learn to transform – might allow the scientific pretensions he associated with his work to be understood in a slightly newer way. This imperative, in effect, borders on what makes for the very singular interest of the practices of experimental science. When the latter are presented as 'rational', as breaking free from opinion or from appearances, they are described with little pertinence. What matters, what makes the difference between success and failure in an experiment is the *transformation* of a phenomenon into a reference capable of obtaining agreement from concerned practitioners.

A 'fact' in the experimental sense of the term only exists when a laboratory apparatus succeeds in overcoming the objections that aim to put this fact to the test, to verify that it really does have the power of creating an agreement between the protagonists. The questions that experimenters ask – isn't there another way to interpret what you are proposing? Are we forced to accept what you claim, or do we remain free to research elsewhere and otherwise? – translate this requirement. The satisfaction of such a requirement does not authorise the 'true' as the final result. What matters is that the 'fact' gives what we will call a 'reliable hold', creating new possibilities to be explored, that is to say, allowing those questions that matter for the experimenters: 'what then?', 'and if?'

As for the categories of the 'object', the properties called 'objective', they will correspond to the questions that the experimental apparatus will have been able to answer in a reliable manner, that resist objections. One will no longer ask what a vacuum is, for example, but one will actively explore all the questions that become possible once one has succeeded in defining atmospheric pressure as a variable the value of which one can bring down. A vacuum? It is something that the perfect vacuum pump would create, but it is also many other things now, as other experimental practices succeeded in getting reliable new holds, succeeded in authorising other questions (the quantum vacuum...).

If we have a dispute with certain inheritors of Marx, it is to the extent that they have accepted (like most scientists, by the way) the image of 'science' as the victory of reason over opinion: Marx would supposedly have deciphered the 'laws of historical development' and the class struggle that is their secret. In so doing, these inheritors have accepted the vignette that accompanies modern science: obey the laws of nature so as to make nature obey, that is to say, to become able to transform it. It matters little to us that Marx himself might have adhered to all that, or that he might never have forgotten what certain of his inheritors have underlined and underline still: that the categories of Marxism have no meaning outside the actuality of the struggle. In other words, that 'classes' have nothing to do with sociological analysis. Marx wrote that the proletariat have nothing to lose but their chains, but it is only when this 'nothing to lose' takes on a signification in actuality and not just a conceptual signification, when a situation of struggle brings them 'into conflict with' capitalism that the definition of the proletariat becomes effective.[3]

Whatever the case may be, what we are claiming goes a little bit further. We cannot inscribe ourselves in the Marxist tradition if we do not prolong in a slightly newer manner the strong relationship that Marx initiated between definition and 'getting a hold'. 'Getting a hold' designates here struggle situations, when the question is coming to grips with capitalism, but it is also what allows one to learn. To prolong is not to criticise, but to pose the question of what the Marxist definition of capitalism, as related to the hold it lends itself to, has allowed us to learn.

And it is here that the rapprochement with the pragmatism of experimental practices matters, because it allows us to think the radical difference between the success that an 'experimental hold' confers and the question of 'getting a hold' on capitalism. In the laboratory, one can bank on the fact that those entities that we call 'electrons' are not in the slightest bit concerned with the hold that allowed them to be defined, nor with the technical and scientific adventures that we have consequently learned to link with them. It is not the same with what Marx defined as 'capitalism', whose strategies are indissociable from the question of hold that it is liable to offer, that is to say, the question of its own vulnerability.

Over the course of the last few decades, the 'disappearance of the working class', the question of knowing if we are dealing with a 'new capitalism' or the same capitalism with a different face, have been abundantly discussed. One might see this as a revealing symptom: the general character of blanket denunciation (it's capitalism's fault) is not, perhaps, simply an unfortunate drift but rather the effect of capitalism having well and truly succeeded in fabricating situations where the pertinence of the hold that Marxist theory designates no longer convinces those it should concern. Certainly one can affirm that this pertinence subsists 'by rights', even if it no longer convinces 'in fact'. From a pragmatic point of view, fact matters: that capitalism has succeeded in evading the hold is what should oblige us to think. To oblige us not to pretend that theory is right and that those who theory no longer succeeds in convincing, in mobilising, are simply misguided.

In fact, it is in order to avoid this diagnosis of being misguided that it is necessary to be pragmatic. Certainly we can understand, even share, the fear of those – and they are right – who sense all the implications of a calling into question of the hold that Marxism offers, of the way in which Marxist theory can guide the reading of a situation, the definition of its stakes, the agreement regarding strategy. But all that implies the success of the hold that it offers, or else it risks becoming a thinking that goes round in circles. If the mobilisation of the 'masses' is posed as primordial, every failure can be explained by the failure of the masses to mobilise, or 'because we didn't succeed in mobilising the masses'. And that is precisely the stumbling block today. Because anti-capitalist militants are then led to become pedagogues and missionaries, enlightening movements that have now become recalcitrant, having different readings of the situation, different definitions of stakes and strategies, of their true interests. And they are equally led to fear every proposition of a different 'hold' as a possible vector of demobilisation, of a loss of confidence. In short, when the hold it defines doesn't succeed, a theory tends to define itself against the world, not to learn from it.

Once again, the temptation to transform a theory into the conquest of a position that is finally rational, supposedly testifying that those who produced it had been able to see through the illusions that imprison others, is not unique to Marxism. For instance, one finds it as soon as it is a question of the scientific spirit, and every time that a scientific controversy is interpreted as opposing those who 'understood' and those who 'still believed'. But this temptation weighs doubly heavily on Marx's heritage. It weighs on it firstly because Marx's thinking is, by definition, a thinking of struggle and not, like the experimental sciences, a mode of interpretation whose eventual reliability might positively interest all protagonists, that is to say, all the researchers in the field in question. For the inheritors of Marx, there are genuine enemies, and to go back on Marx's work is always to expose oneself, or to be exposed, to the accusation of doing the enemy's job for them. And it also weighs on it because the force of Marxism is well and truly to have brought to light capitalism as the master of illusions, succeeding like nothing else in disguising its enterprise of redefining the world in the deceitful finery of progress, freedom, rationality. The opposition between a hold that is finally rational and illusion is thus not a simple ornament but an integral part of the struggle.

That is why we must be very prudent, not so as not to shock our comrades, inheritors like us of Marx, but to guard us against the rocks and other dangers of the depths that are all too predictable. We must recall all those who thought they could conclude that Marx had failed. Some of them went all the way over to neo-liberalism, some became consultants to directors of various sorts, some partisans of an authoritarian state based on consensual values, and some took as the only horizon for their action that of ensuring that unavoidable modernisation takes into account the protection of the weakest and assures the equality of opportunities.

Being prudent here thus signifies first of all not turning the page. We will transpose to the heritage of Marx what the great American pragmatist thinker, John Dewey, in 1922, wrote about the New World, about the United States that he loved and whose promise he saw turn to disaster: 'Be the evils what they may, the experiment is not played out yet. The heritage of Marx is not yet made: it is not a finished fact to be categorically assessed.'[4]

We can consider this experiment a finished fact even less given that the heritage of Marx is not limited to the question of what we have called the 'hold' ... Above all, one must not forget the importance of the work of Marx and others after him, who describe and analyse the strength of capitalism's ability to capture, to redefine and to trick, and the complexity of its relations with modern states. This work precludes any naivety and protects us against the obscene foolishness that today's neo-liberals wallow in when they sing the praises of the market. And it constitutes the most solid of moorings against the temptation to throw the baby – the necessity of constructing an anti-capitalist thinking and practice – out with the bathwater – the errancy of some of those who have called themselves Marxists.

If the heritage of Marx can be analysed in this way, it is because of a rather simple principle. The work that is precious to us might be assimilated to a sort of ethology. An ethologist who is worthy of the name does not try to define the animal being studied, to say 'what' a baboon 'is', for example, but rather to describe and characterise what a baboon is capable of in habitual or unusual, concrete situations. Similarly, the 'ethologists of capitalism' are interested much more in the manner of recognising the beast and its work, than they are in defining it, to say nothing of defining it in a way that would – conceptually at least – assure us of the possibility of beating it. Sometimes their descriptions even make it appear almost invincible. In any case, it is characterised by its strength, not by a vulnerability that would permit the type of hold that is needed to organise anti-capitalist struggle to be thought. Consequently, what must be worked on pragmatically today once again is not the heritage in its entirety, but this question of the hold. How can one 'name' the beast in a way that doesn't make this struggle communicate with the traditional hold, the ideal of a mobilisation that requires that everyone be inscribed in the sole perspective of the 'class struggle'?

Mobilisation: we have employed this term several times already. Perhaps now is the time to recall its military origin. Mobilisation designates the contrary of learning, because the first imperative of armies when they are mobilised is to let nothing slow them down. It is as much a matter of defining the landscape that they cross in abstract terms – there are no longer any inhabitants, cultivated fields or villages, only unbeatable obstacles or possibilities of successful passage – as it is of shutting up those who object or discuss the orders they are given – they are potential traitors as they risk sapping the morale of those who listen to them. It is a matter of 'marching together as one man'. Never, we note, as 'one woman'. Are women (in the sense of gender and not sex) more recalcitrant with regard to mobilisation? We recall reading somewhere that in France, if the execution of women was stopped well before the abolition of the death penalty, it was because certain women refused to go courageously to the guillotine, to face death with the same 'dignity' as men: they would argue, cry, and moan, and this would demoralise the executioners. We wish to be the inheritors of this refusal of woman to agree to be mobilised, to be taken hostage by a superior interest ('behave like a man!').

The question with which we would like to start to take up the Marxist heritage passes via the pragmatic pertinence of the now generalised refusal of a mobilisation that takes people hostage, that requires the renunciation (for a while) of the 'particular' objectives of a struggle, in the name of the common perspective. We must name the beast, characterise its mode of existence, in such a way that a refusal of this type obliges thinking against any transcendence that would feed, even discreetly, secretly, the ideal of a mobilisation. Because that is precisely what groups in struggle suspect when they deal with inheritors of Marx: the double game, with a 'pedagogical' vocation, of tolerant partners who hope and expect that some will finally 'understand' and join forces with them.

In fact, what happened in the course of the last century is full of lessons regarding the ethology of capitalism and well and truly authorises one to ask oneself if the strategy of mobilisation isn't perhaps the worst. After all, to define such a strategy is to indicate to the adversary the way in which it has to mine the terrain, fabricate impasses, put itself out of reach, in short, to invent the means for evading the hold. Consequently, what we must construct, as a hypothesis, is a way to characterise the frightening capacity that this being has of escaping one's hold, in order to take up Marx's pragmatic question, the search for a definition of how, today, it maintains itself and, above all, how it keeps a hold over us.

It is in this way that we want to attempt to prolong the heritage of Marx. If anti-capitalists can learn to approach what the cry from Seattle was raised against in a pertinent manner – that is to say, in a way that creates the appetite for an effective type of hold, and not a taste for veracious denunciation – perhaps they will encounter interested partners, and not lost souls who need to be converted.

4
Infernal Alternatives

Let us take what happens every day. 'Ah, ah, you are cornered' cackle the journalists when they question those who reflect on the political measures of anti-capitalism or who simply want to fight against the closure of a factory, planned layoffs or are demanding an improvement in their pay and conditions. You want a raise? You want to strengthen legislation protecting employees against layoffs? But you will cause factory closures, speed up the relocation process and put people on the dole!

Wherever you try to call exploitation or social hardship into question, you are opposed with the effects that the measures you propose would automatically induce. The possibility of relocating production from a country where labour is more expensive and better protected to a country which is less stringent comes back time and time again in the arguments of the politicians – and the journalists who trot along faithfully behind them. The fact that Europe has been unified without creating a common, obligatory and constraining bedrock for all countries for anything other than the respect for private property, the free circulation of commodities, the elimination of obstacles to competition, patent laws and the like, and has totally refused unification through creating minimum wage constraints and labour laws in general, is proof of 'realism'. One must stop daydreaming. Whatever the fine words about a 'social Europe' they are just sedatives for the use of countries that are still attached to outdated stories of struggles and social conquests. The lot of labour depends on global constraints only.

Correlatively, the new task for those who are now responsible for (good) governance will no longer be to do politics and confront the divergent histories that make up Europe. They will have to explain pedagogically to voters the constraints to which 'we' must all submit owing to 'globalisation'. They will have to explain that nothing can be done against these constraints, because trying to oppose them would make the situation even worse. The unavoidable must therefore be accepted: adapt to the perpetual economic war that has become the only horizon.

'I will explain to you the inexorable constraints to which our action is submitted.' One will recognise the pedagogical style that has prevailed in France since 1983 when the Mitterrand government opted for austerity and modernisation (death to lame ducks, long live our friend, the citizen enterprise). But the general denunciation of these constraints, with the aim of 'opening the eyes' of victims also constitutes a pedagogical enterprise. What we are dealing with is a general reduction of every possibility of doing politics to a pedagogical discourse.

It is in this way that capitalism presents itself to us. Not, to be sure, to the super-exploited workers of *maquiladoras,* to the women or children in the sweatshops of the southern hemisphere, making what we in the north can buy for 'practically nothing'; to us: we who are the inheritors of a history of political and union struggles that have resulted in the creation of states supposed to guarantee 'social peace'. We will give the name 'infernal alternatives' to that set of situations that seem to leave no other choice than resignation or a slightly hollow sounding denunciation. (Such a denunciation is powerless because this situation offers no hold and the conclusion always comes back to the same thing: it is the whole 'system' that has to be destroyed.)

We now find these alternatives everywhere. To adapt, to 'reform' the welfare state has become an ardent obligation. Sacrifices are necessary, otherwise the financing of retirement will no longer be assured. Or social security payments will become a bottomless pit! *Accepting* has become an imperative. Europe has to *accept* GM foods, or it will lose its competitive edge in the global marketplace, and its researchers will disappear down the brain-drain! We must accept the need to keep illegal immigrants out by every means available – let's not be squeamish or there will be a social catastrophe, the collapse of our systems of social security, the rise of the extreme right! We could go on – everyone can add their own examples because the list is interminable. Even the 'veil', the now infamous veil, has become a matter for the 'we have to' that signals an infernal alternative.

One of the signs of the power of infernal alternatives is that we have become used to considering the meritocratic ideal of 'equality of opportunities' as an end in itself. 'If you don't make the most of your opportunities, don't come and complain, you will have got what you deserved ...' Elsewhere, even water, once privatised, becomes something one has to deserve. In our spaceship Planet Earth, with its limited resources, there is no pity for jokers, rebels, mutineers – and if there are shortages there is no pity for the excess mouths to feed and the weak. Those who are not needed, surplus to requirements ... And as everyone who was born since the 1970s has understood, at school and elsewhere: not to be defined as surplus to requirements is something that has to be deserved.

'Once there was a little ship ...', the song goes, and at the end, as the little cabin boy is about to be eaten ('they have to', otherwise everyone will die of hunger), there is a miracle: the Virgin Mary answers the prayer of the little boy, and fish in their thousands leap into the boat, 'ohé ohé'. We are not expecting this sort of miracle, and we think that every time an anti-capitalist struggle can only respond to an infernal alternative with a general denunciation, it is doing something similar to the cabin boy, invoking the transcendent power of the great movement that would make the alternative disappear.[1] Thought and analysis takes a dangerous shortcut here, reaching an impasse over what might allow to *get a hold* on the machine that fabricates these alternatives and extends them out across the planet as a whole. And it is a very bad way of doing politics, because in waiting for the 'Virgin Mary', one limits oneself to denunciation and often to demanding that the state intervene and provide a way out of the impasse – as if it were not involved in the powerlessness to think and invent that these alternatives testify to in the first place.

Of course, the price to be paid is heavy: the tempo of struggles is decided by the adversary, on a terrain of its choosing. Struggle is thus defensive. Its sole horizon is the hope that when 'they' really overdo it, when everyone is forced to understand where 'they' are taking us, the 'masses' will stir. But even if they do, in what landscape, with what resources, carried by what power of thinking and reformulating problems will they do so? 'They are all the same', one will grumble, after betrayal by those who are carried into power and will themselves run into infernal alternatives in turn ...

We took as our starting point a hypothesis: the very mode of functioning of capitalism kills politics. We have just characterised this mode of functioning with the notion of infernal alternatives. Wherever an infernal alternative is constituted, politics gives way to submission, and even those who resist may be trapped, that is to say, may define their opposition in the terms fabricated by the alternative. But we cannot let the matter rest there. The pragmatic position that we have adopted obliges us to put this characterisation into communication with the question of the possibility of getting a hold on capitalism. Not 'the' hold, identified at last, but a hold that might interest those with whom we have embarked. This hold could be said to be that of knowing how to put back into politics what is presented today in terms of an infernal alternative.

The politics in question here cannot, of course, be defined within the usual, statist-electoral co-ordinates. And it does not concern, in the first place, the personnel of the so-called political class: without exception the latter conform faithfully to the landscape drawn by infernal alternatives. It is not a question of denouncing the political class: how could politicians do otherwise if they do not feed on, are not obliged by, are not generated by struggles which concern the way in which problems – always such and such a problem, not the problem in general, and not the 'solutions' – are posed? Struggles – and it is here that the inheritors of Marx can provide precious knowledge and experience – which would be able to (re) create politics where it seemed that there were only technical questions posed under the sign of 'we have to'.

But it is here equally that the denunciation that 'it's capitalism's fault' is entirely counter-productive: it can give the impression that there is only one big capitalist machine, constituted once and for all, which would over-determine everything. A little like 'Society' or the 'Scientific Spirit'. Unless we perhaps create a rupture and engage alongside of all those who have 'understood', we will be playthings of what exceeds us. Now this is to accord both too much and too little to what we call capitalism. Too much, because this is to attribute to it a massive and practically all-powerful mode of existence. Too little, because this is to underestimate the sophistication of the mechanism for which one makes it responsible. If it is a question of (re)creating politics where an infernal alternative is proposed, it is necessary to learn about the means by which this alternative has been fabricated and has taken hold.

When one follows the production of the infernal alternatives whose multiplication systematically kills everything of the order of political choice, the hypothesis that this production obeys a plan comes up against the fact that such a plan would imply an intelligence bearing at once on the whole and on the details, an intelligence that we can't find the slightest trace of when we are dealing with 'capitalists'. To maintain the hypothesis of such a plan signifies that we only ever deal with puppets, manipulated by an invisible Conspiracy/Master Plan.

It is more than probable that there are 'understandings' in high places but we suspect that even there the intelligence required for such a plan will not be found. The production of infernal alternatives seems to function much more on the basis of *moving reorganising fluxes,* which go from the smallest to the biggest: a factory is relocated from France to China, and this relocation in turn has endless effects on the organisation of work itself in France. It is perhaps because of this – and not because of the staggering intelligence of the Grand Conspiracy – that it is so difficult to see things coming, to foresee the way in which they will change the landscape that had been trusted by those who will be confronted with a new infernal alternative.

The strength of capitalism could well be that it is not a centralised system, organised by bosses capable of taking a decision collectively, in the sense that a decision can be weighed up, discussed with regard to its consequences, and also that it can be opposed, turned into a political matter. For the everyday actors of capitalism – from the CEO of a multinational to the modest senior executive or consultant, without forgetting the politicians charged with its 'regulation' – it is always a question, first and foremost, of continuously reorganising its functioning, in such a way as to disempower any possibility of action that might find a reference point outside of the system and its logic.

This was the case, of course, with Taylorism, which served first and foremost to destroy the power held by skilled workers, whose knowledge was necessary in many factories. It is the case today with the management of businesses. One part remains internal, inscribed within the normal structures of the business; and it is for this reason 'vulnerable' to a feeling of belonging to the business, at the risk of making the objective of the permanence of the workforce prevail over and above the 'maximisation' of profit for shareholders. That is why, for one part of the management, big business has systematic recourse to the services of 'management consultants', with 'professionally guaranteed' indifference. It is a recourse for which the immediate justification seems for all that to be a simple matter of 'logic': it is difficult, if not impossible, for those who have their 'hands on the rudder' to see the dysfunctions that need to be corrected to improve the functioning of the business – and to ensure the 'optimisation' of profits for the shareholders.

Taylor is still the patron saint of 'management consultants', and management pursues the work of manufacturing powerlessness. Even direct relations with clients are now directed by software packages that dictate the responses that must be made, without leaving any margin of manoeuvre to employees. These relations are managed from call centres located thousands of miles away from the centres for research and development and manufacture, with whom exchange is no longer necessary. As for the programmers who put the new procedures in place, they work enthusiastically at creating the tools that will allow their interchangeability, that is to say, the becoming stupid of their work.

We could go on. With the new modes of organisation and evaluation of work, the weakness of one member penalises the whole team. Managers are then called on to become invisible: the workforce will do the job of putting things back in order themselves. If need be they can also harass and break individuals. Or in other circumstances one will ask employees to make suggestions (that are very modestly rewarded) in order to accelerate the returns. The best-known example is Toyota, which succeeded in reducing the number of workers in a paintshop from eight to three in four years. And the infernal alternative tightens its grip when a business makes its own factories compete with each other, and makes the threat of factory closure permanent, thus unravelling the whole fabric of solidarity between workers created by the union tradition.

In short, economic exploitation really only defines capitalism very partially. It should be affirmed that capitalism works continuously to reduce the intelligence of its agents, to replace it by automatic behaviour that can in turn become the matter of infernal alternatives. These latter, then, are not imposed by a decision at a global level, they are the fruit of patient processes of fabrication at a very small scale, of careful experiments, because it is always a question of capturing without creating too much alarm, or by creating false alarms. This is all the more effective given that most frequently innovations are not controlled by a plan. They progress and impose themselves, giving the impression that they are natural and make good sense.

What we are dealing with, then, functions in the opposite way to what the apologists of neo-liberalism pretend when they describe a 'natural' mode of functioning, a mode that imposes itself when all the obstacles resulting from our illusions and misunderstandings of the laws of the market are removed. It is a little like science (as it functions in our world, worked over by capitalism): it too is presented as responding to a rationality that imposes itself against illusion, accompanied by the staggering idea of a scientific progress that, like some great monotonous wave, covers everything that exists with its 'objective' intelligibility.

And it is here that the descriptions of Bruno Latour are eminently pertinent. This great irresistible wave is actively, laboriously fabricated by a multitude of local actors who, together, make connections, equipment and operations of translation hold, maintain and support them.[2] One may equally refer today to the work of those who show that if two terms contradict each other, it is 'laws' and 'market', because each particular market is carefully defined, designed, constrained. This not done by a state the intervention of which is defined as thwarting the free play of actors, but by these actors themselves.[3] It is these actors who clamour for the state to protect their patents and brands, to prosecute infringement of copyright, sometimes even to erect barriers round their markets (the prohibition against Americans buying medicine abroad), or to guarantee a comfortable return on their investment (what would the pharmaceutical industry be without reimbursement for its medicines?)

It must be said, then, that the machine that produces infernal alternatives implies entire armies of specialists engaged in the ongoing creation of the conditions of its functioning. Capitalism is perhaps the most complicated and the most difficult of systems, the one that necessitates the most constraints, the most violence, the most effort on the part of public powers, who are led to involve themselves in an infinite number of things, whilst trying to make us believe the contrary. Michel Foucault had warned us about this: control societies require even more minute interventions from the state than the disciplinary societies that they come after.

Correlatively, capitalism will not put up with less state. It cannot, it has never been able to exist, to stand up by itself. There is nothing spontaneous about its growth, it demands a permanent labour on the functions of the state (depending on the conjuncture, certain functions are reduced, others are undermined or dismantled in the name of the market), minute and patient constructions, carefully maintained and revised. It requires a gigantic installation of laws, regulations, constraints, constantly mutating institutions in order to function, the common feature of this installation being to produce the appearance of an automatic functioning, the logic of which escapes political control.

And it is here that struggles which anti-capitalists might be tempted to define as 'merely' sectional (missing the bigger picture...) show their interest. Because they grapple with concrete situations, they allow learning to take place. They may put back into politics what seemed logically inevitable, (re)creating politics in a new mode.

For example, it should be recalled that, amongst other things, during the struggle against GM crops, the eminently partial and incomplete character of the scientific knowledge that accompanied the presentation of the GM innovation became apparent. It was learned that those who presented it as well-defined rational progress to be defended against the irrational perceptions of the public were a bit like the person who looks around the base of a streetlight at night for his keys because it is the only place where there is any light: they were speaking about GM organisms from the point of view of their production in a laboratory. A well-equipped laboratory, certainly, but which, qua streetlight, doesn't illuminate very much: nothing at all, naturally, regarding GM crops, but nothing even regarding what is really done in the laboratory. GM organisms are the product of a rather poor, slavish biology, which knows how to blindly insert sequences of DNA and then has to laboriously sort 'what worked', without really knowing precisely what 'works' means. The struggle around GM organisms undermined the many infernal (rhetorical) alternatives that were hurriedly mobilized, that you either accept GM organisms or you promote irrational fears, accelerate the brain drain, refuse progress that poor, famished countries desperately need... It gave rise to the beginnings of a creation of knowledge with regard to what was considered 'non-scientific', secondary, or irrelevant. And the question of the role of public research and the partnerships that it must now cultivate with industry, itself entered the political arena, to the great displeasure of certain scientists (including some – French – Marxist scientists).

It may equally be recalled that it was associations such as Oxfam who invented an effective manner of doing politics when they helped poor countries take a position in the meetings of the WTO. They were effective because they didn't 'denounce freedom of exchange' but engaged in a dynamics of learning that allowed these countries to resist in a much more troublesome manner. They were able to point out that what the rich countries wanted to prevent them from doing, in the name of the globalisation of the market (that is, the protection of their rural communities), was what they themselves were doing on a grand scale. The failure of the conference at Cancun in September 2003 created an indeterminacy that allowed for a (re)creation of politics where a 'sorry, but we have to' had seemed to impose itself.

Because of such (relative) successes, we cannot stick with the first name we proposed for capitalism – 'the machine that produces infernal alternatives' – it is still too close to a denunciation that would characterize such alternatives as 'false' or 'ideological', liable to be surpassed in one go by the correct analysis, which those interested would then only need to be convinced of pedagogically. In order to create a hold, or more precisely, to design the words that allow the success of those who have created a hold on a situation to be celebrated, we must try to find another way of talking about this production of alternatives that mesmerize thinking. Is it unprecedented? Has capitalism invented a completely original mode of existence? If this is not the case, what sort of 'lineage' does it belong to? It is not a matter here of defining such a lineage in a scientific sense, but of naming it in a way that allows its type of power to be encountered; its mode of influence, what we have to learn to get a hold on, to be deciphered.

5
Minions

We are hypothesising then that if the grand strategy of head-on mobilisation is ineffective, it is because it bypasses what the labour of many thousands of hard-working minions produces, continuously creating and maintaining what then imposes itself with the self-evidence of unavoidable alternatives. Sure they work on a very small scale, whilst infernal alternatives are an overall result. Individually, each minion is evidently incapable of creating the kind of grand alternative that eliminates a whole swathe of politics. But it is through them that capitalist functioning exists in the ungraspable manner proper to it, with – in our countries at least – little in the way of recourse to brutal violence. Usually, the discourse of unavoidable alternatives is enough. It is a discourse that drives one to despair, certainly, but in a way that is well policed, and reasonable (the state 'can't do everything'). Sometimes it is even 'scientific', arising from a science that ratifies these alternatives by adopting the categories that they have put in place.

And it is perhaps all these 'minions' who put us on the right path, who tell us how to name capitalism. Because they do not present themselves, they do not think of themselves, as 'in the service of capitalism'. The question is much rather: do they think at all? One might recall the story of the training of the consultant in the film *Violences des échanges en milieu tempéré*.[1] He undergoes an 'initiation', a 'deflowering' that will make him capable of dealing with the violence of social relations, of fabricating what will engender social misery. He is broken, he has stopped thinking, or more precisely thinking becomes painful and menacing. Other stories about 'deflowering' would be interesting to tell. Those that produced the economists who baptise infernal alternatives as 'scientific', the politicians or the journalists who install them and ratify them, making them into unsurpassable collective ways of thinking, even the scientists who learn to scorn the questions that a 'true' scientist shouldn't pose.

But it is here that we have to pay attention. Pragmatically. Because we know only too well what many readers will conclude: 'I am a minion', 'we are all minions'. That we are all, from the unemployed to the CEO, 'part of the system' is a well-known theme. It has the advantage of being opposed to the selection of 'good' and 'bad', but can also lead to a form of collective guilt that one can rid oneself of only by the most extreme measures: the 'system' is such that only the trajectory of a truly heroic rupture, without any concessions, can pretend to escape from it.

Now, we are certainly, nearly all of us, inside, affected, but we must be capable of saying that *we are not all of us minions*. We must be able to differentiate between the workers kicked out by an operation of 'rationalisation of human resources' and the person who detailed the plan concluding that sacking the workers was a rational necessity. Even if we must resist what seems to be a very lucid, very elevated thought: that of recognising that we are guilty for what we are nonetheless subjected to.

Certainly, those who we are now calling minions are subjected – everyone who is 'inside' is subjected, even bosses – but one must also say that minions, at all levels, from the boss to the secretary, work on the construction of this inside, that they do not limit themselves to applying or following rules, but take pains to apply the rules with loyalty, that is to say, with a certain inventiveness. And they do this even when it is a matter of apparently routine situations. Because what we call the 'system' never functions smoothly: leaks have to be stopped up, escapes blocked, the signification of the rules has to be extended, a situation that is slightly out of the ordinary has to be brought back into line, definitions have to be made to evolve, undoing any possibility of evading them. We all say 'we have to', but the minion says it a little differently, affirming the legitimacy of this 'we have to' by saying 'yes' to it, by eventually finding ways to better enforce it. Minions are enforcers.

To name minions is to propose a pragmatic difference, a difference that must be 'made' because the language that says 'we are all accomplices, we are all guilty' is a poison, and because the search for 'true' accomplices, the 'truly' guilty is another. It is not, for all that, an arbitrary difference. Minions did not vibrate with joy at the cry from Seattle, it made them sneer or suffer, the way you can suffer because of the proximity of what you turned your back on, of what your life affirms the impossibility of. Perhaps they were thrown into disarray when so many users of public transport joyfully decided to 'walk against the market' during the strikes in France in 1995. But maybe they also shrugged their shoulders with an air of slightly tired cynicism: let's wait until everything settles down, if it isn't this government, it will be another that will actualise the necessary 'reform'...

A pragmatic difference is never a judgement but much rather communicates with the question of putting to the test.[2] In the rest of this text, whenever we talk of 'minions' it will always be under the sign of an a priori 'we don't know'. It is only from the type of response given to the test that proposes to think what is being done – disarray, incomprehension, incredulity, cynicism, anger, or 'it would be chaos!' – that it is possible, experimentally, to make the difference between minions and all those who are, of course, part of the system.

It is not, for all that, a matter of denouncing the 'truly guilty'. Nor of describing the victims of a mendacious ideology that would blind them to the truth of what is really happening. Minions are well and truly victims, but victims of a very particular kind, produced by an operation that it is important to characterise.

Naming minions is dangerous. Who doesn't know the passion for the sorting out that can poison a struggle when the question of how it will end starts to insist? When collective enthusiasm gives way to the nearly hateful tension between those who wish to see it out right to the end and others, who begin to think 'we have to'. The accusation 'you are a minion' could be added to the very long list of denunciations. But this danger itself communicates with the question that interests us when we are naming minions, the question of their fabrication: denunciation can contribute to fabricating a minion.

The pragmatic interest of naming minions results from this kind of diagnosis. It is a matter of learning how to apprehend the manner in which a transformation that has little to do with the manifestation of a selfish interest, or a hitherto hidden thirst for power, operates. Accused of betrayal, the person who confirms the accusation by becoming what we call a minion doesn't reveal his or her 'true nature' but has been produced by a 'yes' that has something to do with what used to be called 'damnation'.

That was just one case in particular. The fabrication of minions is a permanent production. It may be 'organised' – as in the case of the 'deflowering' of the consultant – but most often it is diffuse. And it always has something of the initiation about it, with recruitment into the group of those who 'know'. But it is a 'dark' initiation, involving adherence to a knowledge that separates people from what they often continue to feel, and what they now dismiss as a dream or a manifestation of sensitivity one should protect oneself from. The incorporation of the 'we have to' is something of a tipping point, when one turns against oneself and adheres to despair, and it is doubled with a scorn for all those who haven't yet understood, who are still 'dreaming'. And who it is a matter of recruiting in turn. Above all else, minions want fervently for us all to become minions, because they define themselves as 'lucid', and need a world that makes their lucidity right. Sneering 'you still believe that ...', the recruitment of a new minion begins.

The pragmatic question is always one of a way of paying attention. Attention, in this case, to what one already knows but what one might be tempted to refer to the secondary, the subjective, in contrast to the objective characteristics of a situation. Attention, to take another example, to the way in which, little by little, what had been 'won' in 1968 – the possibility and importance of 'speaking' in the workplace – has been suppressed, misappropriated or emptied of its initial signification, that of cultivating the sense of the situation, or envisaging the difference between what one 'has' to do, and what it would be pertinent to do. For the minion, such idle talk is unbearable, and its silencing produces conditions that are propitious to the fabrication of other minions.

The 'we have to' to which minions adhere designates something of the order of the *vindication* of a paralysis. It translates a type of capture that has nothing to do with an idea, mendacious or not. To have an idea is to be able to back it up, to make the case for it, whereas minions are dumbstruck by a prohibition on thinking what they are working for. But that is also what confers on their work its infernal 'creativity'. Humbly but tirelessly they make the regulations, the definitions, the words, the manners, the procedures that will exclude the thinking they find so intolerable. And it is here that we sense that we are becoming capable of a pragmatic operation – 'naming' what we are dealing with, what it is that succeeds in fabricating minions, in making those who it captures active in a way that permits each one to present him or her self as a 'subject', responsible for what he or she does. Naming is not neutral, it is not giving something a simple label – it is a deliberate act that engages a mode of relation or, in our case, of struggle.

It is not in our 'modernised' world that we will find a name that is adequate for the type of hold that capitalism produces as a crucial part of its mode of existence. Modernity has imprisoned us in categories that are much too poor, oriented as they are around knowledge, error and illusion. So as to conjugate the heritage of Marx and the event of Seattle – this moment that didn't change much whilst changing everything, as if a spell had been lifted – we must turn towards knowledges that we have disqualified. There has, for a long time, been a name for something that manages to produce a coincidence between enslavement, the putting into service, and subjection, the production of those who do freely what they are meant to do. It is something whose frightening power and the need to cultivate appropriate means of protection against is known by the most diverse of peoples, except us moderns. Its name is sorcery.

Part II
Learning to Protect Oneself

6
Do You Believe in Sorcery?

Sorcery? It is a metaphor, of course? You don't mean that you believe in sorcerers, in 'real' sorcerers who cast spells, transform charming princes into frogs or make the poor women who have the bad luck to cross their path infertile? We would reply that this sort of accumulation of characteristics translates what happens whenever one speaks of the 'beliefs' *of others*. There is a tendency to put everything into the same bag and to tie it up and label it 'supernatural'. What then gets understood as 'supernatural' is whatever escapes the explanations we judge 'natural', those making an appeal to processes and mechanisms that are supposed to arise from 'nature' or 'society'.

Of course, many will recognise that contemporary disciplines such as psychology, psychoanalysis or even 'theories' more or less coloured by the neurophysiology that claims to define 'mind', are clearly incapable of explaining the effectiveness of that which is called 'sorcery'. But critical good sense will nevertheless insist that one mark a difference 'all the same'! One cannot seriously put the unconscious, neurons and spells on the same plane! There are limits that shouldn't be crossed – notably those that mark the difference between respectable knowledge, however imperfect it may be – and what we know to be simple fictions, objects, in some circumstances, of superstitious belief. A heartfelt cry: sorcery doesn't 'really' exist!

Of course, ethnologists can always intervene and complicate the situation: sorcery exists because it is a part of 'cultural systems'. But they will turn the argument against us by affirming that, in our modern culture, sorcery only exists in a marginal fashion, a belief that is no longer cultivated, a residual survival.

Our approach does not pretend to try to convince ethnologists. The question of the survival of the practice of spells and counter-spells here and there in France is not our problem here. And if we call capitalism a 'system of sorcery', this is not in order to enter into a discussion about the 'correct' definition of such a system. In any case, it is 'we' moderns who have baptised a multiplicity of practices with the same name, who have unified them under the same genre in order then to distinguish between different species, as in biological classifications. And if 'we' can have done this completely legitimately it is perhaps because 'we' – including the ethnologists who have visited the 'others' – stand firm in all tranquillity on the differentiation between what is natural and those beliefs in the supernatural from which we are happily free.

That is without doubt also why the word 'soul', slightly suspect for its connections with the supernatural, has not been integrated into our scientific vocabulary. Mind, psyche, even cognition (and emotion) are preferred. Profiting from this residual degree of freedom, we will restrict ourselves to associating the term sorcery with the risks linked, in popular parlance, with the word 'soul': to sell your soul, to be soulless, to have your soul eaten or sucked out, or captured. And we will affirm that our catch-all interpretations (symbolic effectiveness, suggestion, belief, metaphor and so on) are indeed incapable of approaching the power and craft of thought and action at work in sorcery (which we believe we have destroyed whereas above all we have lost the appropriate means of responding to it).

To dare to place capitalism in the lineage of systems of sorcery is not to take an ethnological risk but a pragmatic one. Because if capitalism enters into such a lineage, it is in a very particular fashion, that of a system of sorcery without sorcerers (thinking of themselves as such), a system operating in a world which judges that sorcery is only a simple 'belief', a superstition that therefore doesn't necessitate any adequate means of protection. But the very naming of capitalism as sorcery transforms the relation with those 'others' supposed to be superstitious. Because thinking that one has no need of protection is the kind of imprudence that, in the eyes of these reputedly superstitious 'others', has much in common with the most frightening naivety: in their eyes, as a consequence, the disaster becomes perfectly foreseeable. The pragmatic risk is to accept the hypothesis of this disaster, that is to say, to constitute the question of our vulnerability and an apprenticeship to the necessary precautions, as a crucial problem.

We really are speaking of 'our' vulnerability, not of human vulnerability in general. Unlike what happened during the period of colonial conquests, capitalism has subjugated 'us' primarily without the use of fire and sword. Certainly the strong arm of the state was never very far away and it has indeed been put to work through persecution, expropriation and repression. But minions, believing they are doing the 'right thing' (together with the great minds and bigwigs who present destruction as a necessary sacrifice, as the price to pay for the triumph of a liberating rationality) have never been lacking.

That, moreover, is why the grand scenarios where human history is placed under the sign of permanent development are possible. As if there was an unshakeable continuity between the moment when the first humanoids stood on their hind legs and contemplated the stars and the conquests marking the modern world. The characteristics of this continuity will of course differ according to the interpretation offered, but in any case it is that of a conquest in which 'we' have perhaps been the actors, but that is valid for the whole of humanity. When we send missionaries, teachers, armies – and nowadays smart bombs or the bureaucrats of the IMF and the World Bank – into distant countries, it is always a work of 'pacification': we aren't destroying enemies, we don't have enemies. It is our backwards cousins we are rescuing – should we really leave them to their fate?

We are not saying that warmongers pose the problem in this manner, but this is indeed how they present it, certain of touching a nerve among their audience. In order to name what they activate, we will speak of unavoidable dilemmas, characterised by so many 'I know, but all the sames'. Unlike infernal alternatives, these do not have to be fabricated, put together by an army of minions. They are always there, always available for the justification of some or other destruction.

And it is not a question of a simple ideology at all, an ideology that would henceforth be outdated because we now live in a 'multicultural' world. Because they touched on certain themes central to this conquest – scientific objectivity and the success of (finally) scientific medicine – the experiences of both of us have put us in direct contact with the 'we know, but all the sames' that mark the limits of this supposed multiculturalism. Or, more precisely, the limits of what we call culture. Certainly there are multiple cultures, each endowed with a richness worthy of respect, but (unfortunately) there is only one 'nature' and it is 'us' who know how to interrogate it, for instance, how to deal with it using medicine that is at last rational.

Each of us can now see and recognise the damages – the eradication of ways of life, ways of feeling and thinking, and the disarray or hate it produces. But how are such damaging consequences to be avoided if we think of ourselves as more advanced than others, the first down a path that by rights is that of all humans. The 'we know, but all the sames' proliferate. How, in the name of a respect for their customs, can we deprive others of knowledge that transcends every culture, since it bears on nature? And how can we respect these customs, if that necessarily implies that that of which we are so proud – to have learned that we are 'all humans' who must be recognised as having inalienable rights – be downgraded to being 'culturally relative'? How can one not hope that others will, like us, learn to make the distinction between the universal – which unites us all, and the – very precious – spiritual supplement of culture?

To place capitalism in the lineage of systems of sorcery is not in the slightest to make it responsible for everything. We are not going to say that aspirin or antibiotics are 'capitalist'. That would be a little stupid and is likely to make infernal alternatives continue to proliferate. But we will say that the manner in which we think about and offer such medicines is indissociable from the very question that set us thinking and daring to take the word 'sorcery' literally.

We have already affirmed that we are not 'minions', not all of us, that we haven't all of us had our souls stolen. But we have to add now that we are all of us vulnerable, in danger of becoming minions. And we are in danger because of the unavoidable dilemmas that we make proliferate every time that we define ourselves – often without even thinking about it – as representing the 'brains of humanity'. Every time that we forget that the very plausibility of our judgements is a translation of the destruction of other ways of thinking and doing. In other words, 'minions' should above all not be opposed to those who 'think'. Certainly the minion makes thinking the enemy, but that doesn't mean that those who aren't minions resisted becoming so because they 'think'. Instead it calls for a diagnosis of what paralyses and poisons thinking and renders us vulnerable to capture.

For the most part, the words available to us trap and are trapped. Most often they turn around the notion of 'ideology', which means that they affirm the possibility of distinguishing between (false) 'ideas' and what those ideas bear on. Thus, behind the lies of ideology, there is a 'good' aspirin, there are 'good' antibiotics, responding incontestably to the 'true' needs of humans. Once the fog of ideology is dissipated, our manner of presenting ourselves and of narrating our history, this history in which we were able to synthesise those molecules that responded to the needs of everybody, no longer presents the slightest difficulty, as peace and the union of men of goodwill reigns.

Ideology connects with the image of a screen, of ideas that screen out, that block access to the 'right point of view'. But the minions – from human resource managers to the scientist denouncing the public concern over GM foods or nanotechnology as the 'rising tide of irrationality' – are not blinded by ideology. It would be better to say, borrowing from the vocabulary of sorcery, that they have been 'eaten up', that is to say, that it is their very capacity to think and feel that has been prey to the operation of capture. To be blinded implies that one sees 'badly' – something that can be corrected. But to be captured implies that it is the capacity to see itself that has been affected.

Correlatively, it is not enough to denounce a capture the way one might denounce an ideology. Whilst ideology screens out, capture gets a hold over something that matters, that makes whoever is captured live and think. To come back to those things of which we are so proud – for example, scientific knowledge, and more precisely those sciences that are inventive and transform the world (we could also take as an example the promotion of the universality of human rights) – each of us can recognise that these sciences play roles that cannot in the slightest be described in terms of the pure advance of knowledge. One may then be tempted to call those scientists who refuse to accept all the consequences of these roles 'blind', only to go on to discuss the possibility of defining a difference between 'true knowledge' and what certain people have called 'the spontaneous ideology of scientists'. To affirm that there is capture instead implies, for its part, a double movement: a suspension and an exposing to risk.

In the first place, then, suspension, that is to say, a refusal to share the 'reasons' scientists give whenever they justify the unavoidable character of the institution of science and its aims. Unsurprisingly, the reasons effectively appear to be grounded in a series of unavoidable dilemmas, some of which have become so familiar as to have started to resemble self-evident anthropological truths. For instance, the so-called 'disciplinary' training of scientists is not designed to produce 'disciplined' researchers – the denunciation would be too easy – even if the price is a highly remarkable submission to the distinction between 'the scientific', which would be their concern, and the rest. This training really aims at toughening up scientific creativity, exacting critique, the capacity to produce objections and propositions.

Many lucid researchers will recognise that this is a matter of a form of mobilisation and that its cost is that outside disciplinary boundaries, simplifying, summary judgements, ideological judgements, one might say, are tolerated, even implicitly encouraged. They will even admit that their scorn for so-called 'unscientific' questions prepares researchers to become allies of choice when it is a matter of justifying an operation that redefines the world. But these lucid researchers will often conclude with a sigh: 'but all the same ... it is the price we have to pay if we want "true" scientists'. Blindness with regards to consequences would be the price one has to pay for disciplinary creativity. The lucid scientist is not a minion but he has been captured by an unavoidable dilemma: if you want creative scientists and not garrulous generalists, you have to accept that they are trained to be obsessive. We aren't going to say that researchers are all minions, but we do recognise here another sort of capture that produces the vulnerability that favours the production of scientific minions. The destruction of the capacity to think, to situate oneself, the paternalistic disdain with regard to questions that are judged to be unscientific, will simply be transformed into a denunciation of the irrationality that menaces the progress towards which researchers work, along with those who respect them.

The 'ideology of scientists' theme no longer works here. In effect it is the way in which scientists are mobilised that creates the distinction between what is judged 'truly scientific' and thus worthy of thought, and what is called 'ideological'. Instead, what can be affirmed is that 'we don't know' what demobilised scientists might be capable of. This 'we don't know' is not ignorance. It creates a question that suspends all evidence-based argument and demands that we accept the need for experimentation, that is, that we risk being interested by concrete situations in which the precarious beginning of trajectories of apprenticeship may be discerned.

Indeed, the suspensive 'we don't know' cannot get an answer independently of the creation of other manners of fabricating the difference and conditions of exchange between a discipline and its environments. Manners that would resist the model of asymmetric membranes that defines a space into which the non-scientist cannot enter but out of which the scientist freely emerges in the name of progress – all the more freely for not 'seeing' the outside as obliging him to think. 'We don't know' thus makes us leave the safety of the regime of judgement for one of risk, the risk of failure that accompanies all creation, the risk of disappointment and also the risk of being accused of 'still believing' in the sciences, of not going all the way (in the last analysis, the hardened soul, refusing to be had, will say 'aspirin IS capitalist'). But mostly what we may be exposed to is the risk of capture, when we ourselves will defend what looked like so promising in terms of 'I know, but all the sames'.

For us, this question of knowing about the risk is crucial, because it is what gives pragmatic value to the diagnosis of sorcery that we are attempting (risking). All thinking about sorcery speaks of the risk of confronting its operations, of the necessity of protecting oneself, because the danger of being captured oneself is always present. Whoever believes themselves secure, whoever believes they can do without protection, marks themselves out as potential victims.

We don't know a great deal about the question of protection, because we belong to a world that scorns it, but in any case we think that we have to learn to protect ourselves from that to which we know ourselves to be vulnerable. This is demonstrated by the imprudent self-assurance of ideology critique, of demystification, of all those who make an enterprise out of the deconstruction of the appearances by which 'others' are had.

7
Leaving Safe Ground

The sense and the vocation that we assign to the inscription of capitalism in the lineage of practices of sorcery does not, then, refer to a new denunciation. Nor is it a matter of a 'major discovery', a putting into perspective by means of which everything would be explained, and thanks to which one could, for instance, say where and when it all began. And nor is it a matter of characterising a unique event. On the contrary, we think that the operations of capture directly associated with capitalism cannot be dissociated from the question of our vulnerability, that is to say, from the other operations of capture from which capitalism profits, that it stabilises, and on which it confers new meanings. But it is a matter of naming what we are dealing with in such a way that the manner in which it has 'eaten up' many of those who have undertaken to struggle against it becomes a matter for thought, and not denunciation ...

When Bruno Latour stated that it is 'we', we who are always so ready to denounce (false) beliefs, who are in fact the real believers – because we believe in the double power of belief and of the critical mind capable of dissipating it – he stirred up a veritable hornets' nest. If you take away the sovereign reference to the critical mind from us, you pull the rug from under our feet. How then can relativism be avoided? Once again, one will recognise here an unavoidable dilemma, the forced choice between the thesis according to which there must be a fixed point on which the lever of critique rests, and the recognition that 'everything goes' (with the menace then that only unbridled relations of force remain).[1]

But evidently the question cannot be one of renouncing what might be called the critical sense, or even the corrosive humour that a Diderot or a Lichtenberg knew so well how to wield in the eighteenth century, before the seriousness of the university put an end to such recreations.

What fabricates the dilemma is not the question of maintaining or betraying critical sense as such but the demand for a guarantee that doubles up with it. Apparently, if we are unable to define guarantees that would authenticate the criteria that authorise critical evaluation, it would indeed be a case of everything goes. A veritable policing of thought and action: if an argument does not claim an authority that should force everyone to yield to it, then it is a simple opinion; if one cannot quantify the value of a landscape that people are struggling to preserve, those who struggle are nothing but sentimental imbeciles. The demand for a guarantee is the demand for a right not to have to take the risk of learning or of hesitating. It is the demand to be able to proceed with the assurance that follows on from the pretension to judge what we are dealing with.

This is why we wish to celebrate the exemplary character of the problematic tension that inhabits the adventure of American feminism (or rather certain of its components). Because in this case there has been an acceptance that there could be no safe ground. Or more precisely that it could no longer be considered such from the moment that the collective experience of American feminists included that of 'women of colour', that of lesbians and of *queers*, bearers of a very different kind of lived experience to that of heterosexual white women. Certainly Simone de Beauvoir's 'one isn't born woman, one becomes woman' provided weapons for a critique of essentialism, of the identification of the lived experience of women with an identity of woman. However, the challenge of having to create and experiment with the possibilities not of overcoming divergences but of living and struggling together with them by transforming them into forces poses a different question. It is no longer a question of critique any more than it is one of finding a neutral position or of putting oneself in the other's place. What matters is to accept the challenge to learn through the test that the other imposes.

It is a fact that many academic feminists have adopted the typically academic position of the demystifying critique, hunting down the symptoms – manifest everywhere, even in the work of other feminists – of the 'naturalisation' of whatever is to be recognised as referring to a socially and culturally constructed gender. They have passed in one fell swoop from the modern position of the critique of appearances in the name of a 'truth' (whatever it might be) to the postmodern critique of everything which might resemble truth. In any case one talks now of 'post-feminism', which is unsurprising, since the word 'woman' may be suspected of conferring an essentialist privilege on heterosexuality (the man/woman relationship).

Evidently to question this move is not to disqualify queer, lesbian, gay, cyber-feminist and other movements. It is rather to question the role that is conferred on them, because this role responds to a typical academic scenario. 'Before, one believed, now we know.' But in this case, it is above all a matter of celebrating the fact that there has been resistance to such a move. There has been an affirmation that one cannot get rid of lived experience in the same way one might throw away a pair of socks, and even less by 'critiquing' it. Women have been able to say that their position engages them in a certain sense 'against themselves', for a future where the experience of women will be different, but in a way that requires an experimental humour, a capacity of inhabiting what one likes differently, not of detaching oneself from it.[2] They do not know what 'women' are capable of becoming but they know that their lived experience 'as women' is both what must be put at risk and what nourishes their struggle and makes of this struggle an individual or collective experiment that is always concrete and never 'finished', never carried out by proxy or once and for all.

Yearning: a word stemming from Afro-American spirituality, which passes from text to text, gives the appropriate tone for this experimentation. It conjugates hope, the plaintive cry and desire, that for which the soul at one and the same time has a thirst and does not have the power to define what it thirsts for. Yearning is something that transforms the soul, not something that defines what the soul has to appropriate.

We have spoken of the cry from Seattle, 'another world is possible!' and we have insisted on the point that it wasn't a matter of demanding that those who understood this cry and relayed it define this other world, that they set out the political programme that would correspond to it. Our insistence is about protecting this cry from the unavoidable dilemmas that short-circuit learning and create the terrain on which infernal alternatives (if you want this, this is what you will get) proliferate. *Yearning* protects the feminists who have been able to resist 'demystifying' critique. Not a fixed point to which one must stick, in the name of which one struggles or utters unavoidable dilemmas, as so many French feminists have unfortunately done, when put to the test by the veil (all the same, we can't tolerate that ...) But a way of disarticulating the putting of backs against the wall, the infernal choices, the despair of dilemmas, by this feeling that the sole things that truly matter are the concrete and risky paths by which what the foregoing had declared impossible could take on meaning.

Whenever one attempts to approach the question of capitalism, as we are doing, there are always two risks, which it might be amusing to describe with words borrowed from descriptive psychiatry: paranoia and depression. To attribute to capitalism the ensemble of operations of capture from which it profits, and to be seized by the powerlessness to resist it.

Yearning protects feminists against paranoia: it does not address a world finally rid of what oppresses it, but a different world. Notably, it is not enough for them to envisage, following the classic formula, a taking control of the wealth produced by all those who produce it, and a reorganisation of production in the direction of the satisfaction of human needs, because feminists are suspicious of every definition of what needs are. The definition of the specific needs of women has in effect always signified an operation of capture. They struggle for a future whose unknowns put them in movement, constrain them not to be suspicious of everything, but rather to put all the 'it is well knowns' on the same plane, demanding for each concrete circumstance a careful experimentation of their consequences and a careful envisagement of how they affect feeling and thought.

Yearning is the cultivation of sensitivity to what makes us vulnerable to the operations of capitalism, without which it would have the fragility of every purely oppressive system. Notably, sensitivity to the 'gendered' dimensions of this vulnerability, for example the mobilisation that implies scorn for the concern for consequences (care), suspected of sentimentalism.

That is why these feminists can resist the depression that is waiting for those who are taken over by the sentiment that the system is too strong or that its victims are decidedly incapable of opening their eyes, indeed, that they desire their alienation. Who conclude, in short, that all this struggle is nothing but utopian. They know very well that what is called 'liberation' has nothing to do with a 'becoming conscious of', or a 'realisation', in the sense that it would be a question of opening one's eyes, of accepting the well-foundedness of an already existing reading of the world. They know the difficulty of engaging in an open process, a process that doesn't put you by the side of those who *have understood*, but which activates the present, making the force for experimenting with its possibilities for becoming exist, here and now.

It is not for nothing that this word, *yearning* springs from the milieu of Afro-American spirituality, from those songs that render present the kingdom that is already in this world. This sense of immanence, which doesn't overcome contradictions but which knows that the sole thing that matters is the event that creates the ability to pass through them, is without doubt one of the gifts to the feminist movement from its women of colour. But it would be a grave misunderstanding to conclude to an 'ancient background religiosity', with the superior tone of the specialists of 'I have understood everything'. Perhaps it would be more adequate to interrogate oneself about this force, which has perhaps inhabited Christianity since the time when it was the religion of slaves, which was rediscovered–recreated by the Black liberation movement, and which traverses today certain elements of feminism, this time knotting together two reputedly disjunct terms, spirituality and politics.

All that being said, it is not a matter of conversion, but of production, a collective fabrication that creates the ability, not, to be sure, of flying away from the safe ground of the commonly self-evident, but of no longer requiring the guarantees that this ground offers to the operations of judgement. The nuptials of becoming and of critique: knowing that one doesn't critique in the name of whatever it may be, but in the very movement by which one becomes capable of thinking and feeling differently.

8
Marx Again ...

We must now come back to the person who, it can be said, 'invented' capitalism, who, that is, was able to name what was in the process of transforming the world, before his very eyes. What ensures that one is never finished with Marx, that turning one's back to him often signifies stopping thinking, is that he didn't see in what he called capitalism a simple situation of economic domination, necessitating a struggle for a fair distribution of wealth. And consequently the question is of course the following: why can the critics of Marxism, with an undeniable plausibility, denounce a Marxist 'economism', a reading that puts economic relations alone in command as the key to all the rest. We know that this question has been discussed a thousand times, it is a matter here simply of experimenting with the changes of inflexion that the 'hypothesis of sorcery' can bring to the analysis.

Such a hypothesis is not foreign to Marx's thinking. Quite the contrary, one could even say that it is the seam that this thinking discovers and exploits. Doesn't Marx show the way in which all categories with a consensual vocation are loaded, from those of political economy all the way to those articulated by the new democratic ideals (human rights)?

These categories are presented as defining a world that one could finally call 'normal', rational and enlightened. No more castes opposed to social mobility, everyone gets their chance; no more oppressive transcendence, everyone is allowed to express and disseminate their opinions freely; no more slavery or extortion of work, workers sell their labour freely and are rewarded as a function of the value that the market impartially assigns to this labour. But these categories make up a fictitious world, a world of abstractions that bewitches thinking and separates it from what is happening, and which has no relationship with what may be associated with justice, freedom and equality.

Marx knew that the adversary, the power that bewitches, that captures the world and thought, had to be named, because to name is to engage in the struggle, it is to assemble a syntax that makes one feel that nothing of what is presented as normal actually is. Besides, it is a classic gesture when it is a matter of fighting off the attack of a sorcerer, a gesture that makes exist the point where one leaves the world normalised by the good will of thought, by the confidence in the commonly self-evident, where one will have to venture into a completely different logic. But it is here also that the fact that of course Marx 'did not believe in sorcery', that he called an illusion what we are calling a capture, takes on all its meaning. An operation of capture poses the problem of its hold, of what it passes via and what it takes hold over. Illusion poses the problem of the truth that is hidden behind appearances.

It is not a matter of saying 'all he had to do was ...' Those who would be tempted to say this should be reminded that what, perhaps, we are now used to, constituted an unprecedented novelty in the nineteenth century: not the temporary but the permanent putting into crisis of everything that holds a society together. Marx describes it in a celebrated paragraph of the *Communist Manifesto*:

> The bourgeoisie cannot exist without constantly revolutionising the instruments of production, and thereby the relations of production, and with them the whole relations of society. Conservation of the old modes of production in unaltered form, was, on the contrary, the first condition of existence for all earlier industrial classes. Constant revolutionising of production, uninterrupted disturbance of all social conditions, everlasting uncertainty and agitation distinguish the bourgeois epoch from all earlier ones. All fixed, fast-frozen relations, with their train of ancient and venerable prejudices and opinions, are swept away, all new-formed ones become antiquated before they can ossify. All that is solid melts into air, all that is holy is profaned, and man is at last compelled to face with sober senses his real conditions of life, and his relations with his kind.[1]

It is no surprise that today's neo-liberals quote this passage with delight, because it is a titanic capacity for reinvention that is being characterised here, apparently without the slightest regret for what is going up in smoke, is being profaned, the destruction of which leaves men sober, with no illusions left. But the absence of any nostalgia for the 'old' world, in the name of which only reactionaries can think of resisting, makes the necessity of getting the 'trick' of the master illusionist, the secret of its power, all the more urgent for Marx. Because the worst thing, what would be truly frightening, would be that no category of thought escapes the trickery that all are similarly produced, made and re-made, incapable of furnishing the safe grounds for a critical judgement. Because if that was the case, the system would have no reliable exteriority, no exteriority that might eventually be capable of destroying it, only pseudo-exteriorities that it creates itself, but which it can, at another time, catch and destroy.

We needed to recall this in order to counter the slightly simplistic accusation of a 'scientistic' Marx. If science – which was supposed to identify the essence of capitalism behind its appearances – was a vital question for him, it is precisely because he had got the measure of the power of capitalist capture. And if it is science that he asked for protection, it is because he had no choice: he belonged to a world in which all the resources for thinking that were not organised as part of the combat of truth against illusion had already been destroyed or were in the processes of being destroyed. It is not that there is an open choice today, but we have learned to discern the traps associated with Marx's solution: we have to leave the safe ground of 'science against appearances'.

Of course one can discuss the question of knowing what conception of science Marx forged for himself until the cows come home. From our point of view, according to which the truth of a science results from the hold that it succeeds in getting, what matters first and foremost is that the strength of Marx's categories, centred around exploitation of labour and the extraction of surplus value, well and truly got a hold. But this hold does not depend on the 'truth' of these categories beyond appearances. Quite the contrary, where these categories are operative, they are all the more pertinent if one recalls that for Marx, precisely because it is defined by a measure, labour power is an abstraction, and that the cost of its reproduction (supposed to correspond to wages) is another. In other words, the qualification of labour power, that is to say also, the cost of its reproduction are conventions that capitalism can make or dismantle.

The operative character of these abstractions, giving a hold in the pragmatic sense, results from how they help us avoid the traps of the 'good will' of thinking, consisting in placing wages under the sole sign of fair or unfair economic exchange. It seems to us that each time that thinkers of 'good will' have sought to substitute concrete definitions for them (seeking, for example, to measure the 'true' value of the workers' competence that qualification would misrecognise), they have lost the protection invented by Marx, because their problem has become one of a form of exchange that it is a matter of making fairer. If only to discover that if one had to provide remuneration for everything that is 'unpaid' (housework, for example) capitalism would be impossible. Not a very profound discovery, implying first and foremost that one has forgotten what Marx knew: the question is less that of knowing what is 'unpaid' but of getting a hold where capitalism pretends to offer the smooth, bewitched face of a 'purely economic rationality'.

Marx's categories 'disenchant', they situate those who think with them outside the questions of the fair and the unfair, the just and the unjust, of what is measured and what ought to be measured. In effect, such questions have no hold on wage-earning as 'social relation' and fall into the trap that consists of ratifying the 'normality' of a society where one buys and sells what can then be defined as 'labour power'. In this sense, the greatness of the heritage of Marx, which we want to celebrate, is – whatever Marx himself may have thought – to have produced a protection against the operation of capitalist capture, to have fabricated a 'bad will' of thought against the charms of economic equivalence.

However, a protection that does not know itself to be such, that is not cultivated as such, becomes dangerous. As soon as Marxist abstractions function as guarantees – that in which one must have confidence, without which one would lose one's hold – they change nature. Instead of making one think, they provide arms for the stupidity of an economistic mode of judgement (economic exploitation becomes the essence and everything else is deemed illusory). Or they nourish the mystique of a proletariat that will finally wake up and understand.

But the temptation of maintaining confidence in order not to lose one's hold is all the stronger given that those who deal with capitalism, unlike scientists, are grappling with what seeks to make them lose their hold, with what has the capacity to 'continually revolutionise [...] the entirety of social relations', and to do so notably in a way that profits from visions, dreams... but also from the categories that attempt to define it. From this point of view, the resistance of the inheritors of Marx to the major theme of the 'new', supposed to have made his analysis outdated, is salutary. That is why, rather than denouncing Marxisms, it seems much more interesting to us to speak of inexperience, the inexperience of those, Marx included, who are led to confuse the legitimate fright associated with the loss of protection that their categories proposed, with a righteous anger in the face of the permanent return of (bourgeois) illusions.

However, to take capitalism seriously as a system of sorcery is also to know that the slightest point of agreement with it, the slightest economising of thought that is offered and accepted, is lethal. Now it is just such a poisonous gift that vibrates in the terrible 'at last' that concludes the passage that we quoted: 'man is at last compelled to face with sober senses'. The defenders of Marx can try to complicate things as they will, the poison is there: capitalism does indeed have a 'progressive' role, it destroyed that which 'misled' humans. In any case, this is what the formidable development of 'productive forces' that it has liberated testifies to.

Of course, the theme of 'progress' is not a capitalist creation, but it could well summarise what has made us vulnerable to the operation of capitalist capture, our adherence to every *mise en scène* justifying destruction in the name of progress (it is regrettable, but it's the price we have to pay ...), indeed to the making of destruction itself progressive. It is this theme that has allowed the sciences to be celebrated not as a creation but as a victory against opinion (it was believed, now we know). It is this theme that Marx picks up on when he disqualifies the social relations that have been destroyed, and it is this theme again which will give capitalism an excess of gratuitous power. All of those who, for one reason or another, refuse a destruction will be thought *and will often think themselves* as 'reactionary', thereby confirming the legitimacy of their disqualification.

From this point of view it is interesting that the Luddites who, at the start of the nineteenth century, tried to destroy what for them were 'machines of the devil', machines for the fabrication/production of misery – those looms that would permit children to do what until then adults had done – have become a reference for certain elements of the alter-globalisation struggle today. To think 'before the Luddites'[2] does not signify that everything that allows for labour saving can be assimilated to the 'work of the devil', but rather the obligation to think against the poisonous separation between what should be preserved, beyond conflict – machines – and what will be the stake of a struggle – social relations.

The fact that Marxists regarded the protests of the Luddites and other combats of the same genre with discomfort and suspicion, perhaps marks what is missing from the heritage of Marx: something that is somewhat analogous to the *yearning* that has protected feminists. Not the (reactionary) condemnation of progress, but the unknown of a world where this progress would not authorise any simplification.

9
To Believe in Progress no Longer?

Progress, in the sense of a supposed matter of consensus, can evidently be distinguished from progress in the sense identified with so-called 'bourgeois states' (and which may be associated with what Louis Althusser has called 'Ideological State Apparatuses'). In this sense, progress is simply a matter of a lie, because these states are not, of course, at the service of common interests in the slightest.

In order to nourish the unknown that we wish to make exist, it nevertheless matters that we do not stick with the denunciation of a lie, as if the truth was accessible to us, as if we were capable of defining the 'genuine common interests', the respect of which would have to characterise a society finally reconciled with itself. The feminists who cultivate yearning have the wisdom to affirm that they do not know, and that that doesn't stop them from struggling. Becoming capable of affirming this 'we do not know', in the case of progress, does not demand (in our countries – not everywhere) that every association between what has happened to us and a 'progress' be denounced as a lie. That would be to denounce in the same blow what has been invented and imposed by struggles to which we are indebted. On the other hand, we have to avoid the trap of a judgement that sorts, that defines 'true' progress, effectively serving 'common interests'.

To avoid this trap, it must first be underlined that capitalism as we have known it so far (in our countries once again) has always needed to inscribe itself in the perspective of a 'progress that would benefit everyone in the end'. And that this perspective needs the state, alone qualified to define the 'common interests' that progress would serve. In other words, the relation between modern states and the definition of common interests is not a lie, it is constitutive. As soon as what a struggle has invented and imposed is redefined in state terms, as responding in a 'normal' manner to the service of the common interest, this acquisition becomes the matter for a double operation of capture, defined by what can be called the 'Statist–Capitalist' articulation.

Characterising the power of capture proper to the state is all the more necessary today as a temptation exists to take at face value the major neo-liberal vindication 'less state', that is to say, to take the horizon of struggle to be the defence of the state's prerogatives, through which globalisation appears to have driven a coach and horses. As if states had not actively concurred in being 'forbidden' modes of intervention that had previously fallen within their responsibilities; as if they had been forced to open up the field to a crowd of hitherto inconceivable infernal alternatives. Yes, to be sure, a certain violence has been used (currency speculation, for example), and capitalism has profited fully from the divisions between states, and today between regions and cities. But it was a violence that was soft, one might say, and which was responded to in the fundamentally apolitical mode of an unavoidable necessity.

Marx has taught us not to confuse capitalism with the heads of (big) business, and one must not, of course – at the moment of calling into question the role of the state –confuse it with elected political leaders, either. The 'pedagogical' objective of convincing those who vote that, apart from the impeccable movements of radicals, politicians are 'all the same' is a rather sad objective: it bets on the disappointment and deception of voters in the first instance, and accepts the same type of definition of the political field as the adversary (making a government fall as an end in itself!), the better to denounce it as an illusion.

But it seems to us that we mustn't expect a 'theory of the state' to provide a reliable political hold, because the question of what the state is, of its role, of what it should or shouldn't take control of or regulate, and how, is not a matter for a (stable) theory: it is what is at stake itself that defines the multiple montages articulating the state and capitalism. Whoever believes that they can in this instance get a hold is always exposed to what one must protect oneself from, the capacity, proper to the state, of 'regularizing', of conferring on a particular montage the legitimacy of rational progress. Today's montage is the result of a radical and ongoing mutation, but one talks of 'reforms'. What is common, on the other hand, to all these montages is that the roles distributed by the articulation of state and capital are not interchangeable. The state does not do the 'work of capitalism' for it. The thousand and one minions of the state can certainly – whatever the definition of the role taken by the state may be since the inception of modern states – be described as fabricating what capitalism needs. They nevertheless respond to different concerns.

In the first part of this book we recalled that far from submitting to the 'laws of the market', capitalism needs the powers of the state as it needs it to enforce the way each particular market is designed. It does not itself submit, it respects nothing, but it has to rely on a 'deal' that allows each situation to be gauged in terms of what it permits, what it promises. And, as has been the case over the last twenty years, it can equally undertake to modify the deal, but it cannot do so directly. To maintain or modify the deal is what it is a matter of *making the state do*. Correlatively, each modern state can be approached starting from this question: *what does it allow capitalism to do?*

Of course, the markets are not sufficient to define the deal. We have learned from Michel Foucault about the immense labour that was necessary to define a 'disciplined' population, the immense army of minions – psychiatrists, psychologists, jurists, criminologists, educationalists, architects, hygienists and so on – who have conspired to produce the apparatuses that produce the workers that industry needs. We also know that, in parallel, something very different was being constructed, a redefinition of the wage relation that affirmed the solidarity of workers, with the creation of the possibility of living without working, if one is deprived of employment, ill or aged, for instance. And finally, we know that over the last twenty years, a new relationship between what capitalism makes the state do and what the state allows capitalism to do has been inaugurated, what Philippe Zarifian calls the 'society of the control of engagement'.[1]

It is henceforth the engagement, the 'motivation', not only of the workforce but also of the unemployed, that mobilises a new multitude of minions of the state. Minions who will affirm with pride that today, progress dictates that it is no longer a question of learning like a disciplined robot or of obeying orders. One now has to 'learn how to learn', how to mobilise oneself, how to recycle oneself in order to merit one's insertion into a labour market that thirsts not only for an abstract force but an engagement of body and soul. Minions who also meditate on new consensual doctrines according to which there are no rights without responsibilities: it is necessary to 'responsibilise',[2] to learn that a right – even if originally it had been conquered unconditionally and for all – 'has to be deserved'.

Control by engagement is not simply substituted for control by discipline: not only do they coexist, but control needs discipline, because the operation of capture here is indissociable from the permanent criticism of the 'rigidities', the perverse effects, the abuses that are put on display as representative of the disciplinary society needing to be flexibilised. Progress henceforth passes via modernisation, rationalisation and responsibilisation – all substantives whose 'progressive' character depends on the continued existence of what 'must be modernised'. In order to become the matter for a new 'progressive' set up, the latter must be separated – in a process of organised amnesia, – from what had been conceived as 'progress'.

This redefinition of progress gives the minions of the state something to hold on to, signifying that it allows the legitimacy that the modern state gives to its action to be maintained: flexibility serves the common interest. But what primarily characterises our epoch is that it is holding up rather badly. During the strikes in France in 1995, at the time when the people were 'finally' in the street, an opinion poll announced that the majority of French no longer thought that the standard of living of their children would be better than theirs. This in itself may well constitute an event where the constitutive relation of modern states with progress is concerned.

We do not speak of an event because it would be a matter of something unforeseeable, a blast of thunder in a calm sky. Quite the contrary, it is rather hard to imagine how the reference to progress could have retained its authority when every day one hears or reads about the perverse effects of technological innovations, the yawning gap between rich and poor, the call for mobilisation and sacrifice in an economic war with no foreseeable term, the dismantling of the social benefits and rights that had come to be taken for granted. If it is a matter of an event, it is because no one can foresee the consequences of the fact that the reference to 'progress' no longer works. And it isn't such and such a definition of progress in particular which is in question – whether it is associated with the market, the sciences, the development of productive forces, human rights or even revolution. It is the order-word that enveloped them all, and which it is henceforth necessary to learn to think without.

It is never very interesting to take advantage of the evidence of an epoch so as to accuse the preceding one of blindness. The challenge is rather to inherit the new hand that has been dealt without accepting the terms of the problem such as it is now posed – that is to say, fabricated again and again in a manner that makes infernal alternatives prevail. And for this, it is not enough for anti-capitalism to evolve: it must learn. That is to say, it is not enough to add 'epicycles', complicated accommodations that allow the essential to be safeguarded, but to create the manner of giving all its meaning to what may demand the putting into question of what was deemed 'essential'.

For example, it cannot be insignificant that Marx wrote, a little later in the *Manifesto* than the passage already cited

> in place of the old wants, satisfied by the production of the country, we find new wants, requiring for their satisfaction the products of distant lands and climes. In place of the old local and national seclusion and self-sufficiency, we have intercourse in every direction, universal inter-dependence of nations. And as in material, so also in intellectual production. The intellectual creations of individual nations become common property. National one-sidedness and narrow-mindedness become more and more impossible, and from the numerous national and local literatures, there arises a world literature.[3]

To express the historical distance that separates us here from the optimistic vision of Marx, we don't see the need to add anything to Félix Guattari's *Three Ecologies*, wherein we find the ravaging of ecological resources on the planetary level, the ravaging, also at a planetary level, of what he calls the social ecology – the capacity of groups to think, create, imagine – and finally the ravaging of the mental ecology, of the capacity of everyone to situate themselves, and to participate in the processes that bring about new productions of existence.[4] One might say that the Marx of the critique of capitalist trickery has won out, historically, over the Marx who believed in a progress brought about by capitalism 'in spite of itself'. The illusory character of this progress is as evident today as the nudity of the emperor. And henceforth another possible end to this story must be imagined: to the clear voice of the child, a horrible silence replies, as if what those 'sober' eyes were contemplating was the head of a veritable Medusa.

The quasi-programmed collapse of what held our societies together, the feeling of powerlessness, of what's-the-pointism,[5] defines a dangerous situation: not a stable passivity, but its contrary, a cold panic, with the possibility that the notions of progress, the servicing of common interests might be consigned to the box of useless props. Fortress Europe is one of the names for this future wherein the epoch when one 'believed in progress' would be defined as finished, an epoch in which immature, unrealistic dreams prevailed. It means a siege mentality, with impotence, cynicism or self-righteousness being mobilised both against an outside defined as menacing and on the inside, against the unneeded, the lazy, the irresponsible and against traitors. And without a doubt, the strong arm of the state, freed of its 'progressive' constraints will give all its meaning to what those in the fortress will demand: zero tolerance.

It is only a possibility, but the fact that it is more than conceivable today marks the fairytale character of the militant perspective according to which 'thanks' to the dissolution of the old worlds by capitalism, humanity is henceforth a 'subject' with unlimited possibilities, a 'subject' that has the means to resolve all the problems which are posed to it. As if, by rights, we were situated on the threshold of a promised land. As if, in order to escape the bewitchment of capitalism, the struggles of today needed to be anchored in a representation of the 'world that we want', a world that we are only separated from by a question of seizing and redefining power.

Of course, one can hold on to such a perspective as something that it is impossible to renounce. It will then be said that the end of the illusions of progress brings us closer to the threshold wherein the masses finally 'understand', the condition of 'true' progress. In this perspective, inhabited by the saving grace of Truth, the 'mother of all progress', the progress which would still be celebrated in a future when all illusions of progress will have been destroyed, is the very progress that Marx celebrated as the gift of capitalism to the history of humanity: to have forced humans to envisage their real conditions of existence and their reciprocal relations with 'sober senses'.

We refuse to share this pedagogical faith in Truth and in a future that is as promising as the present is sinister. We see in this a way of dying with dignity, without renouncing the ideal that transcended the life of those who adhered to it – a *modus moriendi* and not a way of living and creating, *modus vivendi*. For our part we want to think against the fairytale of progress, with or without the Marxists. And to do that, it is necessary to learn not only to *yearn* but also to learn fright in the face of the power of the operation of capture that has made us so proud of our 'sober senses'.

10
Learning Fright

We have presented ourselves as sounding the depths, which signifies, it will now be understood, not a role adopted by 'free choice' from amongst a panoply of other possible roles, but a role that is indissociable from the moment that made us write this essay.

There are many ways of echoing the cry 'another world is possible!' What matters is that none pretend to the privilege of constituting an obligatory point of passage, because this cry, in its abstraction, is faithful to the situation: no more hierarchy, or ordering, designating what ought to unify thought and struggles. There are infernal alternatives everywhere, sure, but each one imposes the necessity of learning, of inventing, that is to say of abandoning the idea that, finally considered from the correct point of view, they will sort themselves out by themselves, in a consensual, and hence apolitical, mode. The other possible 'world' does not designate the challenge of the 'right' form of governance at last, putting the means that have been unjustly confiscated by some at the service of all.

The major lesson of political ecology is that it signifies the impossibility of transcending politics and the end of the separation between the politics that decides on aims and the techno-scientific means that puts these decisions to work. One might say that at the same time everything is politics and nothing is 'purely political', because what political ecology calls into question in the first place are the shortcuts of thought that are dissimulated behind no matter what 'purely'. One might say that it has never been easier to denounce what pretends to 'make up our world' than today, but also that the alternative to which 'another world' alludes has never been sketched out with such demanding and, one might say, frightening traits.

If we felt compelled to take on the role of sounders of the depths, it was certainly not in order to 'frighten', in the sense of demoralising.

Fright, here, rather refers to care, and more precisely to the shock experienced when we have to face the easy, uncaring way we relate to our own power. The answer to fright is not guilt – something we are very good at. Fright calls for creation, for learning how to relate to what our habits and our routines kept at a distance, put under the sign of 'we now know'.

For example, we are in the habit of deploring the crimes of colonisation, and admissions of guilt have become routine. Everybody now knows it was not a matter of civilisation but of dreadful exploitation. But we are lacking a sense of fright when we rest easy with this knowledge, and do not wonder about this 'civilising' enterprise, which we know colonisation was not. Or at the fact that it is not so easy to stop taking ourselves for the brains of humanity, and that with all the best intentions in the world, we may well continue to do so. And that is the case, notably, each time we make there out to be a difference between 'the others', who, in one way or another, are defined by their beliefs and illusions, and us, who see things *correctly* thanks to our sober senses.

Fright may happen when we realise that despite our tolerance, our remorse, our guilt, we haven't changed all that much. We continue to take up all the space, to occupy all the places. When we ask our victims to pardon us, we like to think of them as 'ours', as if the people that we had destroyed were without history, innocent and peaceful lambs, as if we had been the only active powers in a world which merely provides us with the decor for our own crimes. Of course, decolonisation has largely been sabotaged by the putting into place of new modes of exploitation, but how short-sighted and simplistic the slogans that we credited as 'words of truth' were, idealising the victims and refusing to take into account anything other than our own guilt: the right to self-determination or the struggle for national liberation. Forgetting in the process that terms like 'right', 'nation' even 'liberation' are ours, always ours. And finding it normal that our truths should be taken up by those who had been our victims.

How do we make room for others? This is a very practical question and a very painful one too from the moment that the routinisation of good will and of tolerance stops keeping the test at a distance. That is what, for our part, we have learned through our contact with the ethnopsychiatry of Tobie Nathan,[1] which has been the object of many accusations precisely because it confronts our routines with what makes them stand back, scandalised. One can routinely accept the taste and the colour of others, their values, so different from our own, indeed even their 'rationality', so full of meaning, so moving. In short, what we call their culture. But to go from that to having invisible beings, gods, ancestors, the dead enter a consulting room, to listen to them, to negotiate over what they demand, and how they obligate... To go from that to having to accept that the conclusion of these negotiations can collide not only with commonsense but also with our respect for human freedom ... Indeed it is not simply a matter of rituals, with perfumes, music, dancing – very nice all that, very moving – but sometimes of cruel decisions. For example, coming with the parents to the conclusion that a young girl needs to be sent back to her country of origin – whether that is in order to find the necessary protection or to undergo the initiation appropriate to her powers. 'To do what is needed' is not always an easy decision and every well-bred soul will be led to remind us that invisible beings are simple conventions and that one must know how to free oneself from the conventions that demand this kind of thing.

And there you have it: put to the test, our well-bred souls have put themselves in the position, as always, of thinking for others, that is to say, differentiating between those who 'believe' and those who 'know' because of their sober gaze. Even if, moreover, this knowledge has as a consequence the decision that will remove a child from its parents, who are judged to be evidently incapable of looking after her responsibly. What does a pragmatic concern for consequences matter when human rights are in question?

If the truth of an idea is in its consequences, in the type of world that it implies and promotes, we must learn to start from the fright that is aroused by the ease with which our humanist ideals 'good for everyone' (because we are all humans) fall into what might be called a politics of the lost generation. The idea that the parents will be sacrificed but the little one will become 'like us'.

We ought to know now that nothing is less certain than this last conclusion, either at the level of the person or at the level of populations. But we feel ourselves obliged to keep going, otherwise we would lose something more significant than the destiny of this girl or of this population. That is the signature of the unavoidable dilemma. And that is where it is a matter of stopping and looking more closely at what holds us. The question here is no longer 'we know' but rather 'we must', 'we are obliged to'. And it is not a matter of an infernal alternative, concocted by an army of minions, but indeed of an obligation, as unavoidable for us as that which, completely different, dictates that the child return to her country of origin. Perhaps we aren't so different from the others, but there is this one, crucial, difference: that unlike the others, we ascribe what obliges us to an anonymous universality, valid for all, that we have allowed ourselves to be defined by instead of learning to negotiate with. It's non-negotiable!

To accept the idea that our particularity is to have made our 'duties' – that which obliges us but which is also our strength – a universal, all-conquering definition might indeed be frightening. But unlike fear – which leaves us stupefied – fright (if recognized as such, as marking the power over us of what we consider non-negotiable) may make us think. Of course, there is always a way of falling back on routines, by employing categories which as if by chance put us back centre stage, communitarianism, for example. 'Ah we get you, you're pleading for a communitarian politics! But as we know ...' Now, in the case of ethnopsychiatry it is not at all a matter of 'respecting the customs' of a community, of allowing them to sort themselves out, of looking away by affirming that it doesn't concern us. What scandalises so many enlightened thinkers about Tobie Nathan's practice is that it is addressed to people who are there precisely because they haven't been able to sort themselves out, often because they thought that, protected by the land of France, they could escape from the undesirable consequences of their obligations. And that instead of helping these people complete the movement of their 'liberation', instead of helping them to face what binds them with sober senses... this practice that cannot even claim the respect accorded to 'authenticity' seems to have no other vocation than to 'keep them mired up in their beliefs'. The frightening force of such a scandalized *cri du coeur* has contributed to making us sounders of the depths, not trying to define what 'other' world may come into existence but conferring on what we know the force of a warning.

It is neither for pleasure nor because of a taste for experimentation that Tobie Nathan proceeds by way of what obliges those who address him. It is because for him it is the only way to create a situation of co-expertise, where the question of the cure will not be referred to a knowledge that transcends the tawdry finery of culture but would constitute an open stake, which constitutes the patients as explorers and witnesses to their own world. It is not a matter of communicating 'between humans' but of learning to address that which, in a therapeutic situation, can be called a 'cause'. Not a cause in the sense of cause–effect relations but in the sense that one talks of a cause of what makes us think and feel and suffer. For what engages and transforms. And it is here that we must learn fright in the face of any point of view that implies that one can wipe the slate clean of such causes when they cannot be aligned in the great perspective of human emancipation. Certainly, it is possible to destroy them but the sober senses that will be obtained in this way will not be liberated senses but more probably empty or hateful ones.

To think that if another world must come into existence, it will be a matter of articulating divergent causes that no consensual 'common interest' can draw together, is a test. And a test without guarantee, because we can't expect any miracles: there are dangerous causes, frogs that no kiss will ever transform into handsome princes. Of course the great advantage of all the 'communicational' or 'dialogue-based' theories is that they suppose a plane that is 'ready made', by rights having the power to gather together all the protagonists, making manifest what everyone 'should be in agreement' about. They are able to disqualify those who stand as obstacles as proof of ill-will, irresponsibility, even fanaticism. And it will be all the more urgent to take such troublemakers out of the picture given that the urgency of ecological threats which weigh on us all will compel action. Here it is a matter of learning to create the plane where contradictions may be turned into immanent divergences, not in general but on a case by case basis. Because in each case the challenge is immanence, the capacity not to refer to any criteria that 'transcend the plane', that would authorise the security of an overarching judgement.

What is more, we cannot await a possible 'victory' against capitalism in order to accept this challenge – let us mobilise 'against' now, we will have time to learn 'after'. In the first place it is against this temptation that we have experimented with the idea of capitalism as a system of sorcery, capable of capturing those who do not know how to protect themselves. One does not mobilise against this type of power, because it feeds on all the simplifications, all the shortcuts, all the arrogance, just as it has fed on what is nevertheless a part of our strength, which we can't throw away like an old shirt: the relation between 'critique' and 'freedom'. Our strength, what obliges us and makes us diverge, what it is a matter not of denying but of cultivating, in order to give a chance to the cry from Seattle.

To give a chance: as in the time of the Vietnam war, when it was demanded that we 'give peace a chance', but also as in the way that the Ancient Greeks described the *kairos* to be seized, the suspension of the probable, the holding out of a chance for the possible. Nothing more, that is to say, with no promise or guarantee. Nothing less, because it is not a matter of an abstract imperative but of an appetite for new types of risk to be cultivated, also for the production of a memory of what it was in the past that 'made capitalism tremble'. And which those who struggled against capitalism were unable to nourish and protect, because mobilisation entailed the necessity of keeping up a sober sense about everything that pretended to live before capitalism could be defeated.

At this stage of course, the problem is not yet fully deployed. But already what its deployment demands on our part appears clearly: certainly not a renunciation of the critique that sets free, but the inseparability of the process of critique and the process of learning – the contrary of sober senses, a capacity to follow and to create the dimensions that a situation demands in order to escape from the hold of an infernal alternative.

Part III
How to Get a Hold?

11 Thanks to Seattle?

Seattle again, you might grumble. Aren't we giving in to the easy option by referring incessantly to a 'media' and mediated event? And that with an apparent contempt for everything that has happened elsewhere, as if nothing had happened before, no resistance, no refusal of the 'new world order', and as if everything that had happened afterwards 'prolonged Seattle'. Don't we know that, aside from the demonstrations that were explicitly inscribed in the filiation of Seattle, every causal link with what followed can be contested, or at least complicated?

For example, can we establish a causal relationship between Seattle and the fact that since then, new actors have appeared, or that old actors have experimented with new roles, have learned to meddle with what was supposed not to concern them? That, for example, as has already been evoked, during the meeting of the WTO at Cancun in 2003, an organisation like Oxfam was able to give up its humanitarian role and play the role of expert with governments of countries from the southern hemisphere and that the latter were able to stop accepting the habitual diktats of Europe and the United States on agriculture, cotton and the like as their fate? Are we going to say that all that was 'caused' by the anti-globalisation demonstrations that took place outside? Certainly not quite as simply. But where did the strength come from that allowed the besieged protagonists 'inside' at Cancun to escape from the role to which they were assigned? In the same ways as the demonstrations, this escape route is for us part of the event of Seattle. To deny it is to privilege other causes without asking oneself where these other causes draw their power to cause from. In fact, when the experts lamented in the press, pretended that those who jammed the functioning of the WTO 'didn't know what they were doing', suddenly presenting the WTO as the bulwark against savage bilateral trade agreements that it never was, they also testified to the event: they tried to discourage the intruders from meddling with what happens in the court of the powerful, where they have nothing doing.

To write 'thanks to Seattle' is not to affirm a causal relationship but rather to 'give thanks', to affirm one's indebtedness, to say 'thanks' for the chance that has been given to us at a moment when we might be tempted to despair. Of course, it is a matter of a personal experience, but it is also a matter of something a little more significant: to protect the importance of what happened from the acid of the sober senses which will always be right, of course, but whose reasons will always be blind to what they destroy. Blind to the distinction between illusions and what is easy to destroy because it only exists through being cultivated, fabulated, celebrated.

Neither one of us was at Seattle but we want to keep alive a memory of what was in the process of happening at the time, in order to protect the moment against the lucidity that disenchants, and also against the bitter disappointment of those who note that they didn't succeed in changing the world. Because nothing has been won, of course. On the contrary the processes that have transformed the term 'globalisation' into a threat are far from having been blocked. There is no miracle: these processes are not of the type that demonstrations in the streets, no matter how imposing, can stop. But what Seattle put an end to was a veritable sorcerer's spell. 'You can't turn the clocks back', said the European Commissioner, Pascal Lamy, for example, in 1998, when the Multilateral Agreement on Investment was contested. And this was precisely the motto of an operation that had succeeded in disqualifying its opponents as utopian ideologists refusing the inexorable laws of history. It was under the sign of a supra-political legitimacy that the GATT negotiations that put the WTO in place unfolded. The very countries who knew perfectly well what the catastrophic consequences were for them of the Marrakech agreements of 1994 signed them with resignation, as if in this case objecting to them was as vain as trying to stop the tide with a shovel.

We have lived through the installation of this process of acceptance without knowing how to thwart it. We have seen new 'evidence' impose itself, such as, for example, the idea that private enterprise is inevitably more efficient, innovative and intelligently managed than the public sector. Or that every regulation, every collective choice, every political constraint is an obstacle to the 'self-regulation' of the markets and creates perverse effects, whatever the good intentions behind it might be. We have heard, first with laughter, then with incredulity, then with a terrible feeling of powerlessness, more and more voices intone the catechism that social progress can only be the automatic consequence of an economic development that must therefore be freed from any constraint. Even if this means simultaneously teaching the poor to await with infinite patience – as they are at the other end of the chain – the benefits that should follow a development whereby first the rich must get richer. It is even proposed that they be suspicious of what had previously been thought up to help them get out of their situation: *in fine* the real reason for their poverty and for the difficulty they have escaping it is because such help has taken away their responsibility for themselves. Welfare is henceforth a trap for 'social exclusion', the shortening of the working week a measure that increases unemployment and social security contributions (that is to say the indirect salary that reinvented wage labour as social relation) a set of 'charges' that every government has as its sacred and imperious duty to reduce the 'burden' of.

One day the story of the strange passivity of the political parties and trade unions – who not only saw what they inherited attacked but dishonoured too – will have to be told. The story of the way in which little by little a sense of the inevitable settled in: we have to modernise (properly), to 'reform'. Of course there have been strikes 'defending the public sector', but there has not been any invention activating the imagination, which might allow the meaning of what was well and truly in the process of being produced to be made perceptible and felt. There hasn't been any counter-expertise on the offensive, creating new terrains, fabricating new connections, even though the experts reading out the lessons of the new evidence only had slogans to intone. Everything happened as if it was necessary to fight for one's honour defending the settled state of affairs, whilst defeat was inevitable. As if it was already written. As if everybody duly accepted the illusory nature of the idea that it was possible to maintain a social and historical choice resulting from generations of struggle. At least, that is what we felt: the process of destruction was doubled with an effect of stupefaction, a little bit like the rabbit that is paralysed by the cobra about to devour it.

Seattle put an end to that, nothing more, nothing less: not to the process but to the success of a veritable sorcerer's operation of capturing the imagination and the capacity to resist. Once again, we are not saying that the event erupted in a frozen landscape: other movements, other demonstrations can be designated as 'precursors'. But it is as if what took over the streets in Seattle well and truly broke the stupefied paralysis. And in the United States at that, the very place from which all the initiatives grouped together under the heading 'globalisation' seemed to start, and which all of a sudden showed a completely different face.

In Europe, we didn't know that oppositional movements had not only been able to survive in Reagan's America but also to live and innovate, making themselves capable of gathering together the multiple and heteroclite crowd whose uproar broke the cloak of powerlessness. The free press in America did not say anything about it and still says very little. But since Seattle, a generation has learned to break the law of silence that was imposed and another world has learned to sense itself even if it doesn't really know how to move.

The event of Seattle initiated the reopening of a space of possibilities but – just like every other event – it has no other power than that of the continuations that are constructed by those who refer to it. Each time we write 'since Seattle', or 'thanks to Seattle', we are making such a continuation, keeping alive the memory of the time when those who contradicted the inescapable power of the laws of the market were considered as residual remainders of an outdated past. We feel that this memory is precious because we need this resource when the 'true' problem is concerned, that is, the actualisation of this 'other' world the possibility of which was made present at Seattle.

It is indeed the true problem because if it is continued, the cry from Seattle entails grappling with something that, contrary to any and each particular government, will not let itself be intimidated by 'people in the streets'. How could capitalism give up the extraordinary victory that it has won? It has obtained the quasi-general, anonymous, forgetful acceptance that 'progress' requires the calling into question of everything that generations throughout the nineteenth and twentieth centuries struggled to obtain, and had created slowly and with difficulty, including what could be naively believed to have been irreversibly settled after the Second World War, thanks to the guarantee of the state.

The fatalistic feeling has certainly receded: it is not 'laws' that we are dealing with but an army of minions at work everywhere. But it remains the case that the disappearance of the fatalistic feeling will not force this army to disperse like vampires as the sun rises: 'we've been spotted, we've been spotted'. That is why our questions are pragmatic and not theoretical: how to get a hold? But also: how not to lose it?

The choice of celebrating the event of Seattle, against disillusioned lucidity, is part of this pragmatics. That is to say, the choice of attempting to name and to nourish what has provided a hold and has rendered itself capable of making stutter what capitalism had taken for granted. It is not voluntarism – you have to believe in it and grit your teeth against any doubts – but it is a matter of a 'situated' lucidity, engaged by the event, protecting the event, and conferring on it the strength to protect us against what makes us vulnerable, our will not to be fooled.

To protect: that, it seems to us, is the first of the practical issues when one has to deal with what can properly be described, in a perfectly literal manner, as a system of sorcery. The question is indeed: where does 'it' enter? What do we do without even thinking, with the legitimacy of habit and from which 'it' profits? And as it happens, we think that the hold that capitalism has over us could well profit from our (not very pragmatic) idea that the right thing to do when a precarious, hesitant possibility emerges, is to submit it to questioning, to the tests that will have to determine if it has the power to keep the promises that we load it down with. And in particular, if it is has the power to select the 'good' and reject the 'parasites', those who we don't want anything to do with, as well as to demonstrate the delusions of those who have gone astray (one might think of the anarchists of the Black Bloc).

This type of finicky, even malicious attention seems to refer us to a faith in the power of truth to overcome error that goes back a long way in our history (Gilles Deleuze has associated the notion of the Idea in Ancient Greece with a power to select the 'authentic pretender' against its illusory rivals).[1] And capitalist sorcery hasn't stopped profiting from it, because nothing of what capitalism has destroyed was without its defects, its weaknesses, without something for critique to get a hold of and conclude that it doesn't merit being defended. We want to propose another type of attention, one that engages not against illusion but towards a possible. In the insalubrious world we live in, a possible is not to be judged, rather nourished and defended against the voyeuristic chorus of all those who are on the watch, pointing to signs of discouragement or disappointment, taking a rather wicked delight in sighing 'we told you so!', 'we knew it!'. Among them are, probably, those who, before Seattle, derided all who refused to submit with an amused or compassionate 'you still believe that …' But, unhappily, not just these minions – the will not to be fooled is the pride of many serious militant thinkers.

What has to be celebrated then is what could be forgotten. Thus, before Seattle, questions such as 'world hunger', 'the right to healthcare for all', 'child labour', 'third world debt', certainly already existed but their formulation often hesitated between humanitarianism and pure politics. Be indignant, denounce, recruit. They are now starting to leave the terrain of consensual outrage and to be redistributed and reformulated in the form of much more precise stakes. We have spoken of the new role played by Oxfam. The famous Tobin tax is another example. Any such reformulation can be criticised as naive, avoiding confronting the fully unfolded question it addresses, likely to accept compromises. It remains that in such cases an important transition, associated with the learning (again) of nonconformist expertise, has occurred, from the humanitarian concern – with how to limit the damage produced by what it would be vain to resist – to trajectories of apprenticeship that refuse the infernal alternatives and the obligatory slope that they construct and which the future was supposed to slide down.

To speak of trajectories of apprenticeship seems to take us a long way from the image of the 'mass movement', an image that might be evoked by the anti-globalisation demonstrations that have taken over those cities having the sad privilege of welcoming 'summit' meetings. But to write 'thanks to Seattle' is also to propose another image for these demonstrations, that of a heteroclite crowd, peopled with groups caught up in divergent trajectories of apprenticeship, but each of which gives thanks for the presence of the others. Their unity was not that of a mobilised 'mass', nor that of a multitude affirming an 'in common'. It was much rather the unity of a cry, echoing according to heterogeneous significations but conferring on this heterogeneity the capacity to rejoice in itself. One might say that if there has been an event, it is in the experience of this unity making the different components that pre-existed it vibrate together and draw from it new capacities to imagine and to situate themselves.

Heterogeneity is not a defect here, because trajectories of apprenticeship can only be heterogeneous. They must not be confused with the 'discovery' of something that would have succeeded in escaping from anti-capitalist denunciation. In fact, it will always be easy to say 'it was already known' about what is being learned. Yes it was, but only as particular examples, all deriving from the same cause. It is precisely from the poison of this gain in generality that it is matter of protecting the trajectories of apprenticeship. Because one only learns beyond generality, grappling in each case with the infernal alternatives whose construction is always local, even if their imbrication seems to cover the planet as a whole. Each trajectory of apprenticeship is thus 'local', situated by the place in which a hold has been gained. Generalisation is a poison for it, because it risks loosening that hold, proposing a shortcut that would stop the process of learning.

It is not a matter of a pedagogical concern here, that of allowing everyone the time to follow their own paths towards a common truth. Apprenticeship is not a pedagogy, it is a production of knowledge, the production of a new type of expertise, alone capable of destroying what has been monopolised by minions. It is this process that we want to celebrate, that of creating new means of grasping a situation, leading to the production of new ways of acting, of connecting, of being efficacious where the classical protagonists (including unions !) had accepted the problem as formulated by a supposedly scientific and hence 'neutral' expertise. And, in a very interesting reversal of the situation, the minions of capitalism and of the state have then been caught red-handed with veritably fabulous ignorance of the world such as it is: precisely the ignorance that they accused those who think another world is possible of having.

As every hold is local, it is impossible to sketch out a general picture, and we must limit ourselves to the trajectories that we have, in one way or another, been implicated in. Thus we could have spoken of GM crops, or – it's just starting – of nanotechnology. We have chosen the example of the recent misadventures of the pharmaceutical industry.

12
The Trajectory of an Apprenticeship

The pharmaceutical industry has been one of the industries most adept at linking its fate to that of a progress valid for everyone. It could even believe itself to be definitively protected from the calling into question that has affected other industrial sectors thanks to the privileged status granted by a domain of competence on which it practically has a monopoly: the invention of new therapeutic products. Who could confuse it with the manufacture of cigarettes or the sale of arms? Whether they liked it or not, it has succeeded in becoming an obligatory point of passage for all those who were concerned with illness. Even the poorest of countries were bound to see their health situation improve, albeit very slowly.

It seemed that one could only call the pharmaceutical industry into question at the edges, in the details. And it largely profited from this: over the years, it has, without compunction, turned its entitlement to exceptional advantages into order-words, requiring them in the name of the services that it rendered to the suffering of humanity, glorifying in its role in the history of the invention of medicines and in the prolonging of the lifespan of the populations of Western countries. Serving the interests of humanity was clearly beyond political conflicts, a matter of consensual recognition and trust.

It is hard now to understand how Merck, for a long time the most powerful pharmaceutical company in the world, could have been the favourite enterprise of Americans. Today, the popularity of the pharmaceutical industry is a thing of the past and it even has to observe, with disappointment and astonishment that it has become the most detested branch of industry. That is certainly not enough to provoke its collapse, but it really does make it wobble, because none of the strategies that it had relied on goes without saying any longer. As if the ground had stopped being safe and was now littered with traps.

What happened? How did the pharmaceutical industry come to face enemies who don't restrict themselves to denouncing its profit margins but have become capable of calling into question its strategies? The starting point is without doubt the trial against the South African government that started in 2001, on the initiative of 39 multinational pharmaceutical organisations, fully supported by their professional associations. It was with the feeling of a service provided, sure of what was their due, that they opposed the threat of transgression against intellectual property rights for anti-AIDS medication. What South Africa had done to ensure the availability of these medicines at a moderate cost not only endangered the companies' profits, but, the pharmaceuticals said, it was a threat to everyone's interests, because the investment in research would inevitably shrink: infernal alternative.

On this occasion, this argument, which usually works smoothly, collided with groups of AIDS sufferers, who, everyone knows, are pioneers in the kind of apprenticeship process that interests us here. Those who belong to such groups have, in effect, quit their role as sick patients and have succeeded in a double process of the creation of expertise and of the politicisation of what concerned them – research, the availability of medication, the rights of the sick, their relationship with doctors. The encounter was all the more explosive as far from being isolated, patient groups were joined by other groups with other kinds of expertise. Doubtless the corporations could have resisted each of these separately but the coalition was able to pull down the façade of legitimacy, that of the protection of the interests of everyone behind which they were protecting themselves. Some weeks after the beginning of the hearings, the corporations withdrew their action, reduced to chaos.

One could comment on the event as providing confirmation of what was known already: the long list of crimes carefully planned by businesses from rich countries against poor countries and the fact that pharmaceutical capitalism is awash with profits. We should rejoice that in this case a campaign denouncing what had been done succeeded in making it pull back. However, in this case everything would very quickly be reduced to what enlightened political groups knew already and the event would only be an occasion for them to give a renewed consistency and actuality to their denunciations and to recruit new militants. In short there would be nothing new to learn, only a new illustration, a particularly odious one, it is true, of what capitalism is capable of doing.

Now, the case was not closed and the coalition it had united did not disperse. On the contrary, other controversies, which haven't stopped producing new themes for apprenticeship and struggle, have opened up.

In particular, those who saw the threat to all their efforts at struggling against the diseases that ravage poor countries have learned to take hold of and to call into question the new sacred imperative of having intellectual property rights rule everywhere and with no exception. The implementation of this imperative certainly already occupied an important place in the negotiations at Marrakech, but under the spell of resignation in spite of its predictable effects, nothing would stop the infernal dynamic in the process of unfolding, a textbook case of what capitalism can make the state do in the specific domain of law.

For all those on the ground who were mobilised against the epidemic in the most difficult of conditions, the legal proceedings in South Africa thus showed that patents could call into question all their partial successes. There was a concrete, pragmatic apprenticeship regarding patents and how they have become an essential stake for contemporary capitalism. That is also to say regarding the fabrication of a new inextricable association between the power of capitalism and the power of the state, in the very epoch in which the grand rhetoric of the laws of the market predominated, when neo-liberal economists deployed the fiction of 'less state intervention'.

The state is no longer to be identified with nation-states but with institutions such as the WTO, to which nation-states delegate what is to be done, and whose rulings they faithfully apply, in order to leave the new capitalist strategies free reign. In the case of patents, these strategies are of course presented as organised around 'innovation' and they are adorned with the poison of fine words like 'the knowledge economy'. But what they put to work is the appropriation and redefinition of processes of innovation, their signification and their stakes. Capitalism doesn't ask for 'less state intervention so as to liberate innovation' at all, but for new laws, new regulations and legal settlements to be invented and guaranteed by the state. Hunt down counterfeiters, defend our brands, one hears, or you won't have the harmonious deployment of an innovative capitalism finally freed from the fetters of the state, but chaos. And that is what the minions of capitalism don't want at any cost.

We are speaking about a trajectory of apprenticeship, not a tale of victory. The new empire of patents and intellectual property rights is now fully deployed. The 'new deal' has been installed, the new configuration defining what capitalism makes the state do, and what the state allows capitalism to do. Nation-states are henceforth summoned to leave the making of rules alone but they have to enforce their consequences, too happy to be able to hide behind a 'no choice' argument. But the idea of a rational distribution of roles, dropped out of the sky, cannot function as a way of keeping objections at a distance any longer. Beginning with the South African case, a spell has been broken. The anti-globalisation movement has learned new means to address and resist. For instance the pharmaceutical industry has tried every argument to retain its exceptional status as the unquestionable source of human progress, but to no avail. Certain American economists have even dared to ask themselves dangerous questions: if the state is mobilised so as to impose commercial monopolies linked to patents, why doesn't it have, as compensation, the right to intervene in the public pricing of medication?

The question of patents has obviously not escaped from general analyses as a new strategy of capitalism. But general analyses usually give general answers. Faced with the argument of the pharmaceutical industry concerning the rights of poor countries to obtain cheap medication – if you refuse the constraint of legislation on patents and the prices that we are setting for our new medicines, we will no longer be able to finance research into future medication, because 'the profits of today are the medicines of tomorrow' – a general answer could have been: nationalisation is the only true solution. This amounts to taking up the old slogan that it is 'the state's responsibility', a general purpose slogan that signals theorised powerlessness and gives the neo-liberal offensive its target. It was enough, effectively, to highlight all the cases where it could be emphasised that state enterprises don't work (see the USSR for the 'definitive proof') and the total freedom of enterprise could without difficulty again become the only horizon.

If what has been learned since the court case in South Africa is a thousand times richer than any generality,[1] it is because this case gave rise to a dynamic of propagation which activated those who could not wait for a miracle, the final moment of 'all together', without which no 'true' solution would be possible. It was the case with numerous organisations who had until then been defined as humanitarian. It was necessary for them to find the means of immediately opposing the effects of patents that could destroy the reasons for their existence, to deploy an intelligence which was local but which revealed itself to have effects well beyond the point where it was immediately effective.

All those who, in one way or another, were affected by the impact of patents set about imagining very rapidly applicable solutions. In Brazil, even before the election of Lula, this led to the decision to have antiretroviral therapies manufactured by a pharmaceutical enterprise belonging to the state. The director of this enterprise became an itinerant militant, demonstrating, figures at the ready, how the Brazilian solution had enabled the number of people covered to multiply whilst the total budget decreased regularly. In most of the poorest countries, it was materially impossible to imitate the Brazilians, but their example served to mobilise the energies that made the invention of original solutions possible. Thus, one part of the solution could consist of enabling enterprises from countries such as India, which were capable of manufacturing generics, compete with the multinationals. One could, then, even learn to play the market off against the market! Similarly, it allowed for the WHO (which depends strictly on nation-states) to be obliged to change the criteria used to set the list of indispensable medicines, by including certain of those that had already been copied even though they were patented.

Evidently, these 'solutions' are never definitive: from 1 January 2005, countries such as India or Brazil were forced to accept the hard terms of international patent law. Solutions invented in a pragmatic manner are never guarantees. It remains the case that the pharmaceutical industry, which believed itself the best protected, has found itself to be the most exposed. What it feared the most could indeed be in the process of happening: *medicines entering into politics*! That is an event that ought to make sense for all anti-capitalists. Local movements did not serve to 'open the eyes' of those who were 'blinded' by their illusions: they fabricated the problem in a way that didn't exist prior to their efforts. But they did this at the cost of not making their struggle an example of the general struggle against the very principle of private property and the laws that defend it.

The question here is not that of giving up the questioning of these laws, but of insisting on the fact that if this objective had served as the criterion for selecting the 'good' and rejecting the 'bad', that is to say, those who limited themselves to calling into question the way that the industry abuses these laws, then the process of apprenticeship would not have occurred. It is the fact that the pharmaceutical industry claimed the right to trample on the possibilities for struggling against disease by the poor countries that activated the process. And today, this process is working its way back to the rich countries, unfolding new effects. New questions have emerged. For example, how does one explain that the annual cost of medical treatment against colon cancer has increased by 500 per cent in five years? Do we have to accept the escalating costs that make up a bigger and bigger part of the famous (and somewhat fabricated) deficit in the health and social security budget in the name of the medicines of tomorrow?

Evidently it is possible to object that the hold that the abuse allows doesn't attack the problem at 'its roots'. In fact, nobody is naive enough to believe that the pharmaceutical industry has been 'beaten'. But an experiment that continues to be prolonged has been carried out, and its impact is not peripheral at all. Because it is at the very point that the pharmaceutical industry was redefining itself that a hold was achieved and this hold entailed the production of forms of expertise able to make the order-word of a globalisation carried along by inexorable economic laws lose all credibility. Today, the link between neo-liberal globalisation and the harmonious functioning of the market has been undone, and its link with a machine for abuse and destruction, from which no one is protected, has been established.

But what is most interesting is that this link does not define local actors as having at last been compelled to face the world with sober senses, precisely because it doesn't allow things to be understood from 'their roots', where everything often amounts to the same thing. Quite the contrary, it creates actors who learn to think 'with things' against general categories. A medicine is not a molecule produced by human genius, for the manufacture of which capitalism will exploit the workers. The molecule has become inseparable from the way that it is manufactured and distributed, and when it enters into society it is capable of transforming it in multiple ways.

Bruno Latour has called this entrance into politics of entities whose role cannot be reduced to that of a response to human needs, 'political ecology'. Since nuclear power, with GM crops, medicines and many other things, political ecology is invented every time that this reduction is recognised as an obstacle to understanding what the world demands from us.

13
Fostering New Connections

A bringing into politics, maybe, but, it might be objected, one that leaves very little room for political organisations as such, since it is produced by those who, locally – always locally – learn to resist and to create. Is that not a condemnation of the practice proper to politics, caught between a rock and a hard place: on the one hand, all major demonstrations which, one might say, 'open up the terrain', on the other, the 'local' actors that occupy it?

If 'doing politics' remains conceptualised as the necessary raising up of particulars to generality, as the transition towards demands that gather together and are valid for all, that is perhaps the case. If it is conceptualised in terms of complementarity, which signifies existing 'on the same plane' as the raising up of particulars, but a plane that doesn't pre-exist and that has to be created, perhaps it might not be. Because the simultaneous strength and weakness of what we have described so far is that what connects depends on something that is 'ready-made' – pre-existing interests the defence of which is lived as vital. A moment comes, however, when the possibility of and interest in new connections, connections that do not benefit those pre-existing interests, imposes itself.

Thus the interest of which the pharmaceutical industry has been the target has allowed a not very well kept secret to be brought to light. Reading the specialist publications with the attention they required was all that was needed. In fact, the pharmaceutical industry has taken a little while to make the rule of patents one of its primary preoccupations. And if it has only done so since the 1980s, it is because that was when it had to acknowledge that it was entering into a phase of diminishing returns, when the pace at which innovative medicines were brought to market started to slow down.[1] In other words, it is not (only) because of its insatiable appetite for profits that it has given a paradigmatic value to

US law, demanded its international extension, and utilised the rounds of international negotiations between nation-states in the framework of the WTO to ensure that a date of January 2005 was fixed for patent legislation to become obligatory for all member states. It is because it was afraid of the future. It foresaw that when the patents expired on the molecules that have made its fortunes, the arrival of generic drugs would call into question the basis for its profits in Western countries. And so it could not accept that the margins for manoeuvre that its patent rights still guaranteed be called into question in other countries.

A very different landscape has thus opened up. The link that had been constructed between profits made thanks to already commercialised medicines and the financing of research for future medicines was not just the instrument of an infernal alternative whose hold, in the case of a catastrophic epidemic like AIDS, it was urgent to loosen. It was quite simply a lie. The pharmaceutical industry certainly didn't use the weapon of the patent in order to protect the process of innovation. It was to protect against its own (relative) sterility. New questions now pose themselves. Do the sick in Africa have to pay for what the pharmaceutical industry still knows how to do, that is, for copies of successful products that are modified slightly and sold at a premium? Or maybe for the new 'comfort' medicines – waiting for the opening up of the new Eldorado of a 'slimming pill' at last? And should the rich countries themselves agree to reimburse very expensive ('research costs are ever-increasing') variants of generic products without ensuring that they bring a true benefit (beyond a new patent)? It is such questions that organisations like Médecins sans Frontières or Public Citizen address, also raising the issue of a possible financing of research that would not depend on the pharmaceutical industry.

But to occupy this new type of terrain and not limit oneself to denunciation, one must enter the research laboratories in order to learn how researchers collaborate in the invention process, how priorities are determined, how research programmes are elaborated, then selected, how some are abandoned, how finance is obtained, how justifications are constructed at the same time as the projects advance, creating a feeling of ineluctability. Each place that it was forbidden to enter, where it was thought neutral, objective experiments, independent of the uses that would be made of them, were being constructed, becomes a place that it is henceforth imperative to penetrate so as to make expertise proliferate, so as to imagine new ways of financing research, new ways of creating commonality among competences, indeed of rehabilitating excluded competences.

Thanks to the resistance to the business of GM crops, certain farmers have also posed the problem of the 'confiscation' of practices of production, selection and 'improvement' of seeds by specialised public or private institutions. Might practices of mutualisation and exchange that define seeds as a common good not make them capable of doing things that maybe none of them can do alone today but which their ancestors had done for thousands of years? From this perspective, the knowledges and techniques of professional researchers would not be excluded but they wouldn't be in command, 'serving' the needs of powerless and grateful farmers.

In all these cases, the connections do not pre-exist, they have to be created. And their creation might interest certain researchers, constituting the type of test that distinguishes those who put up with the present situation from those 'minions' who would shriek about the 'mounting irrationality' of a public which fears progress. The connection might interest them because they too are 'attacked': the opportunities for research in areas that arise from the biomedical disciplines and from biotechnology (GM crops for example) or the new nanotechnology are directly affected by the new strategies for the appropriation of innovation. The time when these processes could be described – with a minimum of plausibility – by the succession of steps, from 'research undertaken in an academic milieu' starting from questions determined by the interests of research communities, then 'research and development' in an industrial milieu or paid for directly by interested industries, patents at the ready, is long gone. This description was only ever an approximation but today the confusion of genres is the rule (with all the perverse effects imaginable[2]). And – new fact – the definition of what is susceptible of being patented has extended, so much so that the landscape of research questions is directly affected, even determined, by it. Many research pathways are blocked because of already patented steps, and even in the case that researchers get permission not to have to pay for the corresponding right within the framework of their research, what results from their work will fall under the scope of the patent and the research is thus deemed unprofitable.

The Association Française contre les Myopathies (AFM), which has succeeded in fabricating an expertise able to 'enter into laboratories' even at the price of upsetting the 'habits of scientists' has clearly understood this. It chose not to entrust the choice of the allocation of budgets – resulting from Telethon fundraising operations – to the scientists themselves but to leave the responsibility entirely up to representatives from the families of sick children. And it imposed a particular policy on patents in order to avoid the misappropriation by private interests of the research that it financed. Unlike the pharmaceutical industry, the AFM decided to patent on a step by step basis, not so as to realise a 'financial return on its investments' but to prevent the research and innovation from being appropriated by others, the patent thus becoming a means of protection, a little like the case of free software licensed under GNU.[3] All of this had a single aim: to make new therapeutic medicines ready as quickly as possible and at the lowest cost.

However, in the vast majority of cases, researchers were not interested in the AFM's procedure. They were very happy to make use of the resources, adding them to those they were allocated by the state, but they have continued to demonstrate – often under their breath – their rancour at having been dispossessed of the right to choose how these supplementary funds were allocated. They have seen in it a threat to their autonomy: the public is not supposed to meddle with what should be a matter of objectivity and rationality alone. They would have preferred that these funds were allocated to their laboratories per se, not to precise research projects, which imply regular meetings with representatives of the AFM, who follow their progress.

Scientists are used to working with either the state or private enterprise. Here they had the opportunity to start to experiment on the implications of working with a public mobilised as a function of its own interests. And to benefit from this opportunity would also have been a way of prolonging the trajectory of the apprenticeship, for instance of posing, in their own way, collectively, publicly, the question of patents ... before it took hold of them. They would have been able to find there the means not to have to face alone (in the sense of being both socially isolated and in competition with each other) the new injunctions of a state that intends to reorganise their work along the lines of the model operative in the United States since 1980. But so far scientists have resisted an effective politicising of their practices, although they know that these practices are on the point of being integrated into economic strategies. For the moment at least, the majority apparently prefer to cling to the idea that their past role of 'provider' of innovation was well and truly apolitical and to submit with anger, cynicism or despair to what the state lets capitalism do.

To date, the trajectories of apprenticeship that have been articulated around GM crops, which we will talk about now, have suffered the same blockage. Some field biologists and agronomists, whose practices do not generally produce patents, have certainly entered into the trajectory and have vindicated their hitherto neglected expertise as entitling them to intervene in the definition of the risks associated with GMO. But the fact that the primordial interest of GMO results from the patenting of seeds, which is its direct consequence, has not become an issue, starting a trajectory of apprenticeship, for specialist researchers in biotechnology. In a more general manner, it is noteworthy that in France very few researchers protested when – on the pretext that it could hinder progress – the Académie des Sciences announced its opposition to the writing of the principle of precaution into the text of the constitution.

It is in a case like the latter that anti-capitalist political organisations could act: not to denounce, not to generalise what local actors are doing, but to invent the means of relaying and prolonging their trajectory. It would be up to them to recount what was learned along this trajectory, to point out its novelty and scope, and also to pose the question of the connections that are not being made. In this case, that would mean another way of understanding the complaints of scientists: without ratifying the order-word 'science = progress', which means that 'science' would be good in itself, and that the only problem is the usual one of profit-hungry capitalism. It would also mean not affirming that 'everything is connected' but knowing that every connection is a creation, a 'putting into' relation, an event creative of the plane that it will inhabit.

Finally, it signifies experimenting with what getting straight down into the heritage of Seattle means: accepting that if another world is possible, this possibility demands that these organisations must also learn to meddle with what was supposed not to concern them, to quit the role that they have been assigned, which has been assigned to political struggle. But, given the capitalist operations of capture, this implies the creation of other protections than those that resulted in linking the Marxist heritage with progress.

14
Sorry, but we have to ...

Without the anti-globalisation movement, we do not think that the events that made some of the jewels in capitalism's crown today tremble just a bit – the pharmaceutical industry, agribusiness – would have happened. Because such events depend on a logic not of mobilisation but of connection, and the production of connections implies a milieu that could be described as 'activated', recalcitrant or in any case sceptical in the face of justifications which previously 'worked'. Very evidently, as is the case each time it is a matter of activation, a direct causal link cannot be pinpointed. But one can point out transformations, and it is important to do so, for example, the rather striking fact that the public powers have had to abandon their favourite tactic: opposing the democratic consensus to the violence of fanatics (hadn't all their talk in the 1990s been about 'eco-terrorists'?)

With the business of GMOs, notably, it is significant that the press has, in fact, described the way in which the European Commission has set about disregarding the hesitancy of nation-states with regard to the end of the moratorium, in the mode of sad probabilities, without resuming the equation 'biotechnology = human progress' that the Commission itself still uses. The idea that the public is 'against' GMO imposed itself with an astonishing ease, and this opposition is presented less and less as an 'irrational fear' and almost becomes the voice of a 'wisdom' that was on the point of being ignored. And the connections are prolonged, activating new processes of calling into question 'upstream' with regard to that which, accepted yesterday, is now becoming intolerable, like the damage produced by pesticides, for example.

The contrast with the questions that are posed at the level of nation-states, and most notably those concerning the reform of pensions, is glaring. In this case, what dominates is the feeling of fatalism: we have to 'stop dreaming'. Certainly the 'all together' that resounded in the streets of France in 1995 announced something new, which has been confirmed and reinforced by the way in which public reaction disappointed the anticipation of the minions. For them, the French – whose everyday life was disrupted by the strikes on public transport – would denounce all those 'cosseted' public sector workers who were making their lives a misery. And yet, against all expectations, and with a strange cheerfulness, they organised themselves (car sharing) or chose quite simply to walk, and 'to walk against the market', against the fatalism of the reforms that were, it was said, inscribed in the nature of things. However, it must equally be recognised that the minions in the media stopped stammering very quickly and broadcast the image of French people 'refusing to make the necessary changes' – 'lay a finger on their pensions and they're out on the street'. It was a difficulty that subsequent governments would have to confront because the necessity for reform was inexorable. And the fact that anti-capitalist political organisations have seemed to make toppling the government an end in itself has not helped. In short there has been no success in thwarting the unspoken conviction according to which if this government falls, then the following government, or the one following that, would willy-nilly have to pick up the task of necessary reform again until, finally, it is passed.

And yet this necessity is nothing other than that of the conquest by capitalism of new terrain on which to make infernal alternatives proliferate. The ineluctability of a reform of pensions is justified by the predictable process of the ageing of the population, by the injustice constituted by the burden weighing on the shoulders of future generations of workers who will have to support a population of retired workers more numerous than they. The pensioners of the future must therefore agree, from today, to reduce this burden by contributing to stock market-based funds. They must also agree to work longer, in order to rebalance the relations between 'active' and 'inactive'. In Belgium it was named 'a pact between generations'.

But experts pleading for a lengthening of 'active' working life have been careful not to put their 'solution' to the test of under-employment! That would change the nature of the solution they recommend: in fact the real (and probably expected) effect of increasing the age of retirement will be the shrinking of most of the pensions calculated on this new basis. As to those who sing the praises of the pension funds, they are very careful to avoid discussion of the way the funds will weigh upon the workers of the future. Because if the pensions of today are the product of an immediate distribution of contributions, those of 'private' pensions will depend on the profits achieved by the businesses in which the pension funds invest.

The plausibility of the 'yes but we have tos', of the claimed necessity of painful reforms depends entirely on the absence of connections, of a freezing of thought. Finally, it matters very little whether this freezing is submitted to or willed, since the diffuse impression of fatalism, which it becomes more and more difficult not to give in to, is a part of the handiwork of minions. Whatever the consequences. And the consequences are well known. For instance, American pension funds were pinpointed as responsible for the 'rationalisation' processes producing unemployment. As shareholders they put exorbitant constraints on European companies, notably the imposition of an objective of a 15 per cent annual rate of return on their investments, which would be considered lethal for any company (if it does not itself dabble in the stock market). But these constraints, which are pinpointed when it is a matter of explaining the deteriorating conditions at work, the relocations, the reduction in the wage bill, are forgotten when it is a question of the 'ineluctable reform' of the pensions system.

The pension funds presented as a solution by the majority of European states represent a typical case of what they now intend to let capitalism do. Sure it is a matter of letting them get their hands on an enormous mass of capital that had 'unjustly' escaped the capitalist circuits of valorisation, because it passed directly from the hands of workers to pensioners. But it is also a matter of allowing it to make the relations between the 'active' and the 'inactive' a new field for manoeuvre and for infernal divisions. Things are even clearer when pension funds are constituted in a privileged manner with the shares of the companies where the pensioners worked (a fairly frequent occurrence in the United States, with consequences that became public with the collapse of Enron, which automatically brought about the collapse of the pension fund). In this case the connection is direct: the lower the salaries, the higher the profits and the richer the pension fund. The pensioners thus have an interest in pushing for the relocation of their old firm in order to guarantee the levels of profit that the health of their pension fund – and hence the size of their pension payments – relies upon. Even the workforce, the pensioners of the future, finds itself divided between interests that have become irreconcilable: it would be quite logical for a worker to demonstrate against the relocation of the company one day but to approve the move the next, as a future pensioner. Where paying for retirement through redistribution created solidarity between the generations, between 'active' and 'inactive', pension funds are creating a new type of social relation organised around the production from start to finish of an infernal alternative.

But it is also a matter of redefining what it is a matter of making the state do. Pension funds may be an effective instrument for convincing a large proportion of the workforce to delay the date of their retirement, once the size of their pension depends on it. That is to say, an effective instrument for dismantling the collective regulation of the retirement age. The creation of pension funds managed by banks and insurance companies may also eventually result in the redistributive mechanism only providing the social minimum (the basic state pension), as is already the case in Great Britain. All the rest will depend on individual contributions that everybody makes by their own *freewill and responsible personal choice*. Here we have the argument that is at the heart of all the current reforms of what, since the end of the Second World War, has been called the welfare state. From being the result of a collective public decision, the age of retirement has become the product of individual choice, the state having as its task to allow those who will have made the wrong choice to (just) survive.

The situation is analogous to the equally 'ineluctable' reform of health insurance, itself justified by the 'vertiginous' growth in health spending. Once again, as in the case of retirement, the solution that is proposed consists in developing individual responsibility and certainly not in negotiating the collective, political control of spending. The objective of the reforms is to define the contribution from social security in such a way that it just keeps in line with the rate of inflation. It is the additional, personal insurance that should support all future growth. This will allow the price of new medicines or specialist consultations, which had hitherto been fixed within certain limits, to be set by the market ... With the old system, it was necessary to find a way to decide if the collective would accept the reimbursing of a new medicine and at what price. In the new system, it will depend on everybody 'freely' choosing additional insurance. So everyone will choose their insurance policy and the size of their contribution as a function of the risks one 'wants' (or has the means) to be protected against. In its entirety, the centre of gravity of the system will have changed. A collective, public choice will have been replaced by a private contract.

The common refrain for all the reforms of the social security system is the necessity of developing individual responsibility: the freedom and the choices made 'freely' by each of us is the only effective form of regulation. It is also, for example, the justification for the employers' demand to remove any limit to the length of the working week: those who want to earn more by working more must be given the freedom to do so. The old systems of social security have supposedly become too expensive and difficult to manage; they would yield perverse effects that only the mechanism of individual responsibility can offer a remedy for. Real social progress would not be the fruit of collective choices, but the automatic result of millions of decisions taken freely by everyone. I can decide to work more to pay for my annuity, to insure myself against all risks. It is my choice ...

As to the state, which would then only manage social minima, it would also have as its responsibility that of moralising all those who depend on it, making them responsible individuals. Is it not legitimate to impose a form of tutelage – usually reserved for people who are incapable of looking after themselves – on those who make the 'wrong choice'? Is it not also legitimate to verify that they deserve the help they are being given? The logical conclusion is that it will be up to the unemployed, the sick, the injured to be able to prove that they really have done everything and are continuing to do everything to extricate themselves from their situation, and thus merit the state's help. The distinction that becomes important here is this: it is between those who want to help themselves, and the others. With the underlying idea that those who really want to extricate themselves will always manage to. But to demonstrate this, it is imperative to reduce help to the minimum in both amount and duration, so as not to encourage those who aren't looking to help themselves. Such a system is steeped in psychology. Its logic leads it always to set up more and more controls and to create indicators to justify the rejection of those who aren't sufficiently deserving. The minions busy themselves.

We have painted this picture in order to give a measure of the problem: why have we resisted so badly? How could we have allowed the idea that it was better to put our fate in the hands of blind private interests, to give up on any possibility of collectively defining what would merit the name 'progress'? Because the absence of new connections doesn't explain everything. What has imposed itself is in fact a disconnection. One may have had the impression that we had arrived at a point where no one really knew any more how the redistributive system of pension and health-care worked, nor what differentiated it from the new systems proposed.

In France, during the struggles led against the reforms in 2003 and 2004, it became clear that one of the principle tasks should be to learn this anew, to re-appropriate collectively what had not been protected, as it had been taken for granted. It was no longer a shared knowledge but the privilege of an administration, a knowledge inscribed in codes, categories and regulatory definitions. And those who were charged with managing the system in the name of workers have shared in this amnesia. When at the end of the 1980s, what had been conquered as an 'indirect part' of salaries started being described as a 'burden', a handicap in the race for competitiveness,[1] there was no outcry. The new order-word had been launched successfully: who wouldn't want to lighten the 'burden' of the 'employment costs' that weigh on 'our' employment-producing businesses? The logic of the 'burden' of costs is that one should do everything to reduce them, whilst for common sense, the logic of a salary (direct or indirect) is to increase. So, the words weren't neutral but they prepared for the reforms that were intended to transform into a private matter something that for previous generations had been included in the political sphere.

Disconnecting so as to reconnect differently, whilst producing powerlessness among those who will suffer the consequences of this operation: this statist–capitalist feat is what made us decide to speak about the sorcerer's operations of capture. For us, such words would perhaps be able to transmit, effectively and affectively, what had happened, what is happening, and which can't be explained by the weakness of individuals, their cynicism, their selfishness or their beliefs (such explanations themselves participating in the sorcerer's operation). Words that cannot be pronounced without the indissociable obligation of thinking the production of collective means of resisting.

15
Reactivating History

If we had been able to relate how the collective means of resisting the 'necessary' reforms in our countries are in the process of being produced, maybe we wouldn't have had to adopt the position of sounders of the depths. Maybe the process would have made us into adventurers. We would have experienced the apprenticeship of what it is that we think these means demand, an apprenticeship that those who only trust 'action' have often thought they could do without: learning the antidotes against what has poisoned, and continues to poison, the situation. And the poisoner here is, in the first place, the state. The state has never promised us anything because, unlike the politicians, it doesn't have a mouth with which to make promises, but demands that we place our trust in it, as if it were keeping a real promise. We are poisoned as soon as we address it as if it was a matter of not betraying its promises.

The poison was already there when workers mobilised so as to protect their 'entitlements'.[1] They called upon the state not to betray, not to go back on what had been settled. But the dangers of the word 'entitled' are that it communicates with 'obtained' rather than 'invented', and that the struggles that imposed this invention, that created what had until then been inconceivable for many, get forgotten. The scene is then ready for the reply 'sorry, it can't be afforded any longer'. It is the reply of a father to his children when he has been ruined or made unemployed. It is also ready as a way of calling on the public as witnesses: 'look at the selfishness of these people protecting their entitlements: all they can say is "you can't touch this, we're entitled to it!" How will we make France/Britain/Germany etc competitive with such people!'

It will be protested that these are only words, but words make one think or block thought. The word 'entitled' puts the state in the position of guarantor, or demands that it take this position. And from the moment that entitlements are respected it delegates to the state all responsibility with regard to solutions. What is worse, it actively discourages the questions that make connections, as such questions might discourage the logic of mobilisation that the defence of what has been gained makes prevail.

For example, can one legitimately ask about the quantity of medicine consumed in a country like France (three times higher than in the Netherlands)? According to the logic of the protection of entitlements, that is to offer grist to the mill of those whose project is precisely to ration the consumption of medicines. The ready answer will thus be: how dare you speak of over-consumption at a time when the poorest families have more and more difficulty getting treatment? There is a sort of limit here on the questions it is licit to ask: at a time when we are under attack, one must close ranks in order to be credible and effective. Nothing must complicate the demands and protests that will bring people 'all together' in the streets. The cry 'all together' certainly possesses a strength, a joyful potential. But it is for us a matter of learning to defend this strength, this joy, against every form of mobilisation that would prevent connection and cooperation with local experiments, those of patient associations, for example, or of those doctors who participate in the journal *Prescrire*.[2] or even with certain social security or mutual insurance workers. It is a matter of defending strength and joy against every form of mobilisation that would inspire mistrust towards all those places where one thinks 'too much'. If it is not protected, the cry 'all together' is quickly transformed into an incantation.

Other words communicate instead with the necessity of re-appropriating the stakes that have been entrusted to the experts of the state (or rather to recognized 'experts' in general, since experts in unions are now trained in the same way as their colleagues paid by the state and conform to the same kind of reasoning). These words will encourage entering somewhere we were discouraged from going, where things were not meant to concern us. For example, the labyrinths of the allocation of the massive budgets managed in health insurance. Isn't too much being spent here and not enough there? How can doctors be helped to resist the pressures of the pharmaceutical industry? How can responsibility for the aged be managed in institutions so that they aren't stupefied by the prescription of drugs? How does one give oneself reliable means for weighing up the value of the new, very costly molecules that appear on the market? Can we imagine new means of financing research? Who should be brought together to envisage this? Which other questions should these problems be connected to? Which counter-expertises should be created?

Such words necessitate another way of telling, and so inheriting from, our story. We have allowed the logic of the state to rob us of it. Of course, many of those who obey the mobilisation organised around the logic of 'the state's responsibility' remember that in France, social security, as organized after World War II, was not solely the fruit of a state decision. It was born from the 'nationalisation' of an institution that already existed: the mutuals [les mutuelles]. But that's a bit like a prehistory: what was created, what was thought up with the mutuals is now the object of dead memory not of a shared, living culture. As if the state had entered into its legitimate role by nationalising this invention.

Past history doesn't count much if the objective is that the state continue with its protective role, if the whole of the struggle against reforms takes this objective as its horizon. On the other hand, it does count if the question is that of connecting with what the state appropriated by making it its concern, that is to say, by imposing its own modes of definition on it. And it is then a matter of resisting a 'rationalised' history, a history that explains itself, transforming the defects and weaknesses of the mutuals into so many justifications for their taking in hand by the state. That's the story that the state tells, a state that has never looked kindly on an autonomous organisation that aspires to do without it, to not function as one of its organs. A state that sought out the opportunities to control. Already, under the Second Empire it arrogated to itself the right to nominate the presidents of the mutual societies. This is generally 'forgotten', because in this case, the state eventually had to retreat. But that took fifty years.

When it is a matter of nineteenth-century Europe, it is the history of the creation of the unions and of political parties that is remembered. But the idea that one could oppose a form of association that would function according to the principle of 'from each according to his ability to each according to his needs' to a devastating economic system, one destructive of all the old bonds of solidarity, has had at least as much importance. The first intellectuals of the worker's movement were unanimous in seeing their ambitions for what could be a different, socialist, society, summed up in such a principle. But far from being an abstract wish, referring to a brighter future or a utopia, it was a principle that could be put to work immediately, in the form of mutual societies, the most famous of which was that of the weavers of Lyons. The functioning of these societies was opposed to that of the insurance companies of the time, because in the case of insurance companies, one makes a contribution on the basis of the risks against which one wants cover, for a cost that is independent of income. Without counting the fact that in the case of the mutual societies, there aren't any shareholders to pay.

Once again, it is not a matter of idealising this history, of depicting the mutuals as all and only good. There were some very good reasons for bringing them under state control, besides that of ensuring the extension of the system to everyone, that is to say, of transforming the mutualist reinvention of the wage-relation as a general positive model. What we want to underline is that this 'victory' also brought into line a creation of the workers' movement that did not correspond to the logic of the state resulting from the revolution and put in place by the republic. What we want to propose to those who would describe the nationalisation of the mutuals as a remedy that was made necessary by certain deviations is that maybe, as Péguy would say, pride made us take the last resort for perfection.

The French Revolution put an end to the different forms of property and of organisation that stratified social spaces. Now there would only be the individual, henceforth the citizen, on one side and the Republican State on the other. Several laws – like the Le Chapelier law – proscribed all intermediary forms of property and social organisation. Among these, common lands, lands that had not been appropriated, rather given up to the use of everyone, should be counted. These forms of non-property, which were a collective means of preventing social misery and which one finds in diverse forms in all unequal societies, are often called 'common goods'. Such common goods have often been threatened, but they were literally caught in the pincers of the articulation of state and capital and destroyed. Marx even gives the *enclosures* movement, the suppression of the English *commons*, a key role in capitalist development. And yet, in this case, he couldn't reconcile himself with identifying a form of capitalist destruction with the removal of an obstacle to socialism. Questioned by a Russian revolutionary about the character, progressive or not, of the abolition of the Russian commons that were then under threat, Marx seemed to hesitate and finally opted for the necessity of defending them as a support for a socialist society.

One might say, then, that with the mutual societies, the workers' movement, in its constitutive phase, invented in its own manner a space of common goods that, retrospectively, is not without analogy with those that have been eradicated. Except that this space was willed, designed and conquered: it is a creation of means *immanent* to the condition of wage earners, which would combat the distress of social misfortunes and ensure that workers who were injured or sick or too old, and could no longer work would have an income. These new common goods were forms of collective property that did not attempt to locate themselves radically outside the capitalist environment. But like the

English *commons*, which landowners blamed for being an obstacle to the endeavours of productionist rationalisation, they can be 'blamed' for having withdrawn from the circuits of 'valorisation of capital' the flows of money that capital is attempting to recuperate today.

In effect it is indeed because of the very manner in which it collects and operates the distribution of wealth that over the course of time mutualism succeeded in partially redefining the wage relation and made it enviable for other social categories, something that was really hard to imagine in the nineteenth century! However, that doesn't signify that this reinvention of common goods in itself possessed sufficient strength for its becoming to be indifferent to the manner in which these goods would be managed. On the contrary, its own weaknesses and above all the history that followed its nationalisation show that it could only be maintained or developed on condition that it was cultivated, accompanied by, and rendered capable of burgeoning in new initiatives.

A trace of this history – nowadays referred back to an outdated prehistory – remains in France in the quasi-unanimous and ritual formula: 'Social security must not be brought under state control' ... even when that is exactly what is being done! Because the state has become an obligatory point of passage. It is to the state alone that it falls to make the system obligatory, to impose the deduction of a portion, now called indirect, of salaries, and all change will henceforth have to pass through state decision and regulation. The 'nationalisation' that produced social security marks a great moment, a moment of triumph, and at the same time, the creation of the precise point where the state can at last intervene, can influence the system, make it submit, redefine it.

Since it was put into place, an unstable montage has thus been created: on the one side, a system depending *de facto* on the state, on the other, mutuals reduced to a 'complementary' role, tempted to function more and more like private insurance companies. Certain mutuals will retain the principle of a contribution dependent only on income and with the same rights open to all (this is the case for the first of them, the *Mutuelle generale de l'Education nationale*). Over the years and after many reforms, many will choose insurance-based schemes (one chooses the risks against which one wants or – more likely – can afford to be insured, and on which the size of the contribution depends). But the history of the system itself soon took on the appearance of a gradual hold-up (in the name of progress): from management by the elected representatives of the wage earners, we passed in 1967 to co-management, which gave half the seats on the administrative councils to employers, before doing away with elections altogether (the last took place in 1984) and recommending that management be entrusted to a senior authority made up of 'independent experts'.

The story can then be told in a new manner. Intentions and reasons don't matter much. The republic has well and truly succeeded in absorbing an intermediary form of property. It has succeeded, that is, in producing amnesia among the inheritors of the invention of the mutual, who become 'anybody', beneficiaries of 'entitlements'. Today, whenever 'social peace' (which the state still has as its duty to be the guarantor of) changes definition, because it is a matter of allowing private interests to take over what the mutuals had protected from their grasp, the anybodies are called on to go out into the streets, indignant of course that someone dares 'lay a finger on the Sécu', but having no other power than that of this indignation.

We aren't judging. We are not saying that it was wrong to make the system obligatory, any more than we are saying that those who agreed to confer a paternal, protective role on the state were conniving with the amnesic logic of alignment. And nor do we want to oppose subjective good intentions and objective complicities defined from the point of view of an overarching knowledge. We are only saying that all of us who have benefited from the heritage of the mutuals didn't know that we had to continue creating it in order to protect it from capture. This capture took place as soon as the management of the heritage was defined as a 'technical' problem, beyond politics. It was not disputed because we, or our parents, trusted in the state instead of learning how to 'give thanks' for a story of invention and struggle so as to become capable of prolonging it. We let what had become obligatory become 'normal', the responsibility of expert minions, without cultivating the other dimension of the term obligation, beyond the state: that which makes us indebted, what forces us to think.

There is a lesson in this story that has the value of a definition, in the pragmatic – that is to say, consequential – sense of the term. This lesson bears on the asymmetry between the intentionality proper to what we have called a system of sorcery and the (sometimes) good intentions of those that it captures. This asymmetry refers to the obstinate work of minions taking advantage of the temptation of having confidence in the state – a temptation which we may know to be misplaced but which is almost irresistible.[3] As a result the amnesic normality that is established with 'allowing the state to take charge of' is turned into a poison. Correlatively, the sole thing that may allow for resistance to capture is a demanding process of fabrication, of connection, of the creation of new problems.

That is why we think that Gilles Deleuze guessed right when in 1985 he took the risk of not abandoning the terms 'right' and 'left', which at the time were often mocked. Rather than disowning them, which can lead straight into the trap of 'neither left, nor right', or which suggests the purity of a new beginning, he 'recreated' them by affirming that between left and right, what mattered was not the difference in convictions or values, but a 'difference of nature'. The 'left' only exists to the extent that it learns how to resist what it is enough for the 'right' to take advantage of. 'The left, Deleuze wrote, really needs people to think', and its role, whether or not it is in power, 'is to discover a problem that the right wants to hide at any price'.[4]

Part IV
Needing People to Think

16
A Cry

'Needing people to think.' We hear this as a cry, inseparable from this other cry, 'another world is possible!' It seems to us that such cries are effective in making us feel the mass of renunciations, the 'we have tos' that separate us from what Deleuze calls thought.

What does 'people' – whose 'not thinking' makes us cry out – designate? It isn't only the innumerable minions of capitalism or the state, it can equally be those who denounce them. It can concern everyone, you and us. In any case, it excludes no one, least of all 'thinkers', those certified to think. It may well be all of those who claim to think 'in the name of the people'. As if, all things considered, the fact that it is necessary to 'represent' those who 'don't think' was only a secondary problem in relation to what takes precedence: that those who don't think accept that the one they recognize as thinking in their name is right, is their 'brain'. 'To need people to think' is the cry of someone who knows, who feels him or her self to be living in a poisoned, ensorcelled, poisoning and ensorcelling world. And knows that the question of a proposition being right or not cannot be separated from the question of this proposition needing or not needing the people who are concerned by it to think.

In any case, that is why we think that one must refuse to pass from the cry 'another world is possible!' to a programme describing 'this other world that we want'. Because this programme would have either to appear utopian or to take no notice of the primordial unknown of every situation: the difference that the event by which 'people' seize hold of a problem that concerns them can create. And it is indeed a matter of an event, not of the restoration of what would be a sort of general right, about which one might ask what would hinder it, what can 'prevent people from thinking'.

That is also why we don't like theories of alienation, haunted by the fact that 'people' seem incapable of 'becoming conscious' of the truth of their situation. Whoever poses the problem in this way is supposed to know a bit about this truth: he doesn't need people to think, rather, he regrets that the truth that he possesses, and which should by rights be valid for them, doesn't enlighten them. When we proposed to identify the mode of existence of capitalism with that of a system of sorcery, it was not a matter of giving alienation a different name. We have tried to pose the problem, not in the diagnostic mode that separates those upon whom it bears from the person who makes it, but in the mode of a pragmatic diagnosis that is inseparable from the question of adequate means.

The difference that matters thus passes again via the power of words. To theorise alienation is to use words that are made more for the use of those who pose the problem about others, than for communicating with pertinent practices (one, monotonous, solution only: 'becoming conscious of'). It's a bit like psychiatrists, whose diagnosis fills up hundreds of pages in the DSM,[1] but whose means of intervention are desperately monotonous: pills and therapy. On the other hand, to use the name 'sorcery' is to use a word no one can utter with impunity, keeping at a distance from what is diagnosed. It is to initiate a process in such a way that its truth does not derive from the agreement of specialists, but from the manner in which the diagnosis obliges whoever makes it.

'To need people to think' first of all implies paying attention to the words that allow whoever claims to think to do so without needing the thought of others. The word 'victim' is one such word: to the extent that one is dealing with 'victims', it will be a matter of defending them, often – and in the first instance – against themselves. Of course, to defend the *sans-papiers*,[2] for example, as 'victims of a policy that is criminal', is in itself perfectly legitimate. But it is not particularly 'leftist' in Deleuze's sense. That is to say, in the sense that it is a matter of not accepting situations such as they are proposed to us: always poisoned, always leading to infernal alternatives.

Let's pose the question differently: what have we learned about the *sans-papiers*, after the remarkable mobilisation to defend them? How have we learned with them to think what their migrations imply? Have they become, for us, members of *particular groups* having their own histories and projects, with whom one must be able to negotiate, so that they can be received with dignity, rather than an anonymous group defined by a constant of the state? A migrant from Mali is not at all the same as a migrant from China, as those who have devoted their efforts to supporting people in irregular situations well know. But the question is political, it bears on what this knowledge is susceptible of producing. As long as we do not learn to define migrants other than globally, as 'without', we will be doing without these questions. We will not feel their need. That is also to say that we won't need them to think, to feel entitled to stop presenting themselves only as victims.

Of course, there is worse – when we bracket together with the label 'victim' people who do not present themselves as such. Yesterday it was the consumers of illicit drugs but more often it is, not surprisingly, women. Prostitutes or girls with the veil, who it is a matter of saving – in spite of themselves, should it be necessary. They are victims to such an extent that everything that they affirm can be considered null and void. There are some rather obscene texts where people supposedly on the left 'refuse to support the argument for freedom of choice', which, it is supposed, covers up the 'social dynamics at work'. These are the words of a judge, of one who knows and who will, with death in his – or, unhappily, her – soul (a soul that will perhaps, before long, be captured) demand or undertake to apply a regulation or a law. The question is not at all that it would be necessary to submit to the argument for 'freedom of choice', to accept that the 'it's my choice' are words of truth. The question is the unavoidable dilemma that poisons thought: either to bow to their freedom or to understand the argument of free choice as a manifestation of their difficulty in recognising that they are 'victims'.

We are talking here about 'us', not about those we have called the minions who construct infernal alternatives; about 'us' in so far as we are vulnerable to the capture that produces minions, even while we might present ourselves as struggling against the injustices of this world. That is why Deleuze's cry, the 'need for people to think', is addressed to all of us, whether we define ourselves as 'on the left', or denounce the betrayal of 'the left', or affirm the vacuousness of this term.

But 'to need to' doesn't signify affirming that in a situation in which 'people aren't thinking', one must abstain. Rather, it demands that all the words, all the justifications that would ratify the manner in which this situation is then characterised, be avoided. It is a matter of succeeding in making this fact exist: that the words that characterise such a situation only hold up by default, that they profit from the event 'becoming capable of thinking' not taking place. It is a matter of resisting, doubtless, but not only in a way that gets the fact that the problem is badly posed accepted (that is easy enough). In the first place and above all it is a matter of no one possessing the definition of what the 'true' problem would be – because that needs 'people', those who should be the protagonists of the problem, to think.

Black American feminists have posed the question: 'Can the house of the master be dismantled with the master's tools?' This is a crucial, tormenting question, because the response cannot be summed up by a simple change of tools. Masters, our masters, do not draw their power from one tool in particular but much rather from a definition of the tool, from a relation to the tool, which makes of it a neutral instrument that is indifferent to the hands that handle it, designating all its users as interchangeable. Thought, in Deleuze's sense, poses the same problem. It is not the 'same thought' regardless of whether it ratifies ready-made categories with a consensual role, stemming from unavoidable dilemmas and infernal alternatives, or is interdependent with trajectories of apprenticeship, which are always local, never generalisable as such.

In order to name this difference, we will borrow the distinction that Deleuze and Guattari have proposed between 'majority' and 'minority'.[3] Every thought, every position that counts itself 'normal' and that defines every divergence as a divergence from the norm – that is to say, as what must be explained (she thinks like that because she's a feminist) – is majoritarian. Groups to whom it would never occur to think or wish that everyone would follow their example, are minoritarian. We say that every thought defining itself as valid 'by rights', independently of the fact that the people that it nevertheless concerns are or are not capable of thinking, and every tool claiming to be 'neutral' with regard to this difference, for 'anybody to use', are 'majoritarian'. In both cases, the thought or the tool are marked by the type of economising that allows a situation and the people who are concerned by this situation to be understood independently of what they think about it, as the means may be understood in terms of the end that is defined for them, but without them.

Here, then, majority does not pass by way of number. A group can be minuscule and majoritarian – it is enough for it that the themes it proposes be defined as, 'by rights', valid for everyone. Correlatively, if what Deleuze and Guattari call a minority does not dream of becoming majoritarian, it is not because it selfishly cultivates its particularity, but because those who belong to this minority know about the link between belonging and becoming. Contrary to becoming conscious of, the experience of becoming does not bear with it the dream of its generalisation. Those who have known a becoming-mountaineer or mathematician do not dream of a world filled with mountaineers or mathematicians. If they think of others, it will never be in terms of 'anybody', but rather of other minorities, with whom connections, encounters and alliances would be possible, which don't homogenise the heterogeneous but give to each one new powers to act and to imagine. To fabulate.

One can understand here the scope and the limits of the role of the sounders of the depths that we are seeking to play. The only general statements that can be made bear on what poisons us. We cannot respond to the 'big questions', notably those that preoccupy the inheritors of Marx. We do not have any grand theory, but we do have the concern to find the words that are able not to crush the present under the challenge either to have to find a substitute for the working class or to contribute to its awakening. We only know that the discourses that have depicted this working class as a great force free from every milieu, every attachment, defined by an immediately universal calling, that is to say, by some intrinsic 'good will', have imprisoned us in the categories of fidelity or betrayal, taken us hostage.

We haven't got the time to waste with the poor substitutes that are proposed these days, with 'citizens' or 'civil society' promoted to the status of an immense source of wisdom and answers. Schools today, to whom our dear little brown, blonde or red-haired children are entrusted for so many years, are discovering that the minimal, reassuring and consensual type of citizenship that it was their responsibility to produce, could only be produced in the past thanks to a shared confidence in the future, progress and merit. Without this confidence, from which they benefited without being able to inspire it themselves, they no longer know what to do. Majoritarian self-evidence made out that the production of people able to think, was 'normal', a simple matter of good (pedagogical) will. The idea of a thinking, responsible and disinterested citizen, the figure of an inalienable legitimacy that today is supposed to have been confiscated (but which it would be enough to recuperate), is a rather uninteresting fiction.

It is not, for all that, enough to denounce the lie, as if the truth could be deduced from it. There isn't any symmetry between the truth and lies when the truth cannot be dissociated from a becoming. Every majority, even if it is a matter of a quantitatively infinitesimal group, always defines a situation starting from generalities that exceed it, and that is why it always fabricates hostages. But becoming is never produced 'in general', by the liberation of hostages. The obligations that give to a situation its power to make think are not decreed, they are cultivated.

17
Interstices

The distinction between the majoritarian and minoritarian poses the question of the modes of calculation of problems that can be associated with the state. The question arises even if this state cultivates the pragmatic art of particularising problems, as has long been the case in the Netherlands: in the past, it was possible to envy the supple intelligence of the Dutch state faced with the appearance of new problems like that of drugs.[1] Even in this case, what is delegated as the state's responsibility is always redefined by the state in terms of its own perception. And the categories of state perception always signify a putting out of play of minoritarian dynamics, a putting outside of politics of situations. That is why the degree zero of politics, its majoritarian form, is the demand that the state fulfil its responsibilities. One never puts a situation into politics without knowing that one is 'doing' politics, because quitting the degree zero is to pass from a position with a neutral, majoritarian vocation to that of the minoritarian construction of a problem.

One should never trust the state. However, in the unhealthy milieu that is ours, this generality is not sufficient and one never pays enough attention. At every moment, oppositions can arise, backs can be pushed up against the wall, the separation of the pure and the traitors can appear as an obvious necessity. Thus, if one identified 'not trusting the state' with the imperative 'only one path to salvation, that which escapes the state', every definition of a situation would be taken hostage by this general imperative, the most formidable of all: that which arms those who are adept at purity. That is why we like the image of the interstice. An interstice is defined neither against nor in relation to the bloc to which it nevertheless belongs. It creates its own dimensions starting from concrete processes that confer on it its consistency and scope, what it concerns and who it concerns.

What an interstice is capable of is an unknown [*une inconnue*], except that the notion of the interstice calls for the plural. The beauty of the science of materials is to have rendered the great relations of cause and effect undecidable in the case of materials, because it has learned to address them as the milieu for interstices, for faults, or fissures. The question of knowing what a material is capable of when a tension is applied to it – recovering its original form, remaining folded, breaking – depends on interstices, but no interstice has in itself the power to cause anything. Effectively, the interstice doesn't give any response, but it generates new questions. And these questions – for example, where does an interstice stop? Where does one encounter the indifference of the bloc to what pushes through it? – do not have a general response, one independent of the concrete processes that define the bloc as a milieu for interstices. It is this undecidability that interests us, because it is opposed to the a priori judgements that would dismember minoritarian dynamics under the blows of unavoidable dilemmas 'either ... or ...' To pose such questions is to learn to think 'by the middle'.[2]

Thus, before the intervention of the 'self-help collectives' of users of illegal drugs, enlightened specialists could correctly affirm that the question of drugs was only a symptom, that the 'true' problem was poverty, exclusion, discontent in the banlieues and so on. They were 'right' of course, because their reasons allowed them to denounce the mendacious character of the anti-drug crusade that mobilised police, psychologists, social workers, judges and even 'thinkers', grand interpreters of what taking drugs (illegal ones, of course) signifies. But these reasons also communicated with the identification of the interested as victims, not as protagonists of a situation which was theirs.

In France in the 1990s, when the associations 'Limiter la casse' and 'Auto-Support des usagers de drogues' (ASUD)[3] were created, when 'drug addicts' characterised themselves as 'unrepentant users of illegal drugs', not as victims but as *citizens like everyone else*, the deal changed. Not laws, sure, but the 'milieu', the manner in which these laws are lived by many protagonists: they stopped being self-evident and were envisaged as productive of most of the effects to that point attributed to drugs and used to justify their prohibition. A process of apprenticeship could begin, that bore on what mattered to those who this process had become capable of gathering together. And this process, as quantitatively minoritarian as it might have been (the majority of 'addicts' obviously weren't participating) contributed to a transformation of the way many therapists and social workers dealt with any 'addict' (if some can, then we are obliged to think them all differently). It gave them a hold where they had been subjected, where they were defined by sad 'we have tos' and in danger of transforming them into a creed, the creed of the 'minions'. In short, one of the effects of the interventions of the self-help groups has been to show that one can be wrong in being right, when being right, describing the drug problem as 'only a symptom', follows from a majoritarian view that abstracts from the question of who is posing the problems and how they are posed.

We are talking of a problem 'that gathers together', not of a problem to *be resolved*. Because one of the most deathly generalities is the confusion between the fabrication of the problem and its solution, such as is demanded by those who ask 'but what are you proposing?' Whoever poses this question situates themselves in the 'bloc', because it is a matter of asking the interstice, often with good will, what will allow it to be closed up again. However, not answering the question from outside but learning how to produce it in minoritarian terms at the heart of the interstice is part of its fabrication. If not, there would be a disjunction, the taking of hostages, a sorting out of the 'pure' and the potential 'traitors': between those for whom all that counts is the difference to be maintained between the interstice and the bloc, and those who will be suspected of aiming at or accepting the closure of the interstice. What matters is the creation of manners of doing and thinking that resist the imperative of having to reply to the question in the terms by which it is posed, manners that aim to keep alive the memory of something very simple: in general there's every reason to be wary of whoever poses such a question from the outside. The state may well be all ears should this happen – but it is emphatically not the receptive ears of a good father from whom one would expect understanding, to whom one would owe loyalty.

It is not for all that a matter of defining the state as the 'enemy', lending it a coherence, a personality that it doesn't have. One always has to deal with functionaries working under the imperative of the 'we have to', but not all of them are 'minions'. Tested by the existence of an interstice, that they may help or crush, certain of them are capable of hesitating, of being infected by a precarious sense of the possible. It is at once both a chance and a trap. One must never trust in the good will of those who are and remain agents of the organs of the state, but to put them up against the wall, to ask them openly to betray, is to contribute to turning them into 'minions'. It is to exclude, a priori, the existence of possibilities of creating that are always precarious, always to be thought and never 'natural'. Possibilities, that is, of fabricating an intelligence of the heterogeneous as heterogeneous, where each term is the occasion for the other of experiencing his or her position a little differently.

A politics of interstices should therefore refrain from any general judgement bearing on the difference between interstice and bloc, between the 'true' interstice and those that have been 'recuperated'. The fabrication of each interstice creates its milieu, the manner in which its 'interior' and its 'exterior' are distinguished, at its own risk. The trap that one calls 'recuperation' designates the moment when the outside redefines the inside on its own conditions, and does so under the domination of 'we have tos' that ratify the common, majoritarian norm. But it is not enough, for example, for an association to receive support from the state for it to be condemned as 'recuperated'. Certainly it can be, most notably if the progress reports then demanded by the public powers, instead of being the occasion for an intelligent and deliberate keeping at a distance, become the moment when one must give an explanation and bend to the kind of account that the state demands. What was an interstice has then become an 'organ', giving the state new possibilities for perception and action. But the question of the progress report can itself become the matter of a successful political fabrication. The interstice has then been the occasion that provides the test that succeeds in creating a difference between zealous 'minions' of the state and those who, thanks to it, have the experience that it is possible for them to become part of the process in their own way – here, accepting a report they know is 'fabricated'. And that without having to make a heroic choice, the imposition of which takes hostage and allows the 'pure' and the 'damned' to be opposed.

Interstices are often born from a rupture, but they can also be born from an operation of repair. Let's take the example of what can today be called the 'GMO event', that is to say, the fact that in the case of genetically modified organisms, the anticipated consensus, founded on the order-word 'techno-industrial innovation = progress' has been held in check and contested politically. Certainly one can affirm that the 'citizen conferences' that were inaugurated on this occasion had as their prime objective the repairing of damaged credibility, to 'reassure' and restore consensus by recognising the legitimacy of concerns and the necessity of taking them into account when 'managing' innovation. It was not seriously a question of making what concerned the stakeholders[4] only, those who represent the true, that is, truly blind and selfish interests that define the innovation in question, a matter of public debate. It was not a question of allowing the 'irresponsible' to interrogate the manner in which agricultural production in our countries is defined, for example, or the consequences of this definition not only here but elsewhere, in countries whose 'development' we are supposed to wish for. To reassure the public, certainly, but above all not to pose a political problem.

The fact remains that some have turned this operation into an opportunity, resulting in the 'discovery' that, if they are consulted in a way that doesn't presuppose reactive passiveness, 'ordinary citizens' are well and truly capable of posing awkward questions, of giving up the role of uninformed worriers that had been attributed to them. A very interesting interstice has opened up in the bloc of sociologists professionally dedicated to the role of interpreters of the 'public perception of risks'. That is to say, in cruder terms, to the role of specialists distributing the various ways that the public has of 'imagining' that there are risks, according to the relevant parameters. Certain sociologists took the opportunity of a study of the perception of risk to put to work consultation apparatuses able to favour the processes of the construction of positions and questions, thus breaking with the definition of a science that has to 'explain' public opinion in terms of influence, habitus and relations of domination.[5]

It will be said: what can a few sociologists do against what is on the horizon? Against what will close up the interstice that might be opened up by the discovery that citizens are capable of constructing a position? Because what is indeed predictable is the professionalisation of the consultancy processes, with the reign of blind procedure – the procedures have been followed, so the result is legitimate. A new generation of minions is being prepared, those who will be the 'co-ordinators' who will 'responsibilise', who will 'structure the debate', who will 'promote consensus'. We say that those who object in this way contribute to the closure of the microfissure, to the perpetuation of the anti-politics of the probable, against the political creation of the possible.

The Chinese seem better able than us to 'think by the middle', if their proverb 'the madman pulls up green shoots, the wise man weeds around them' is to be believed. The madman here is the person who evaluates and judges, forgetting that he is a part of the milieu, and that condemnation, scorn and derision are so many sure-fire ways of undoing what is, in a vulnerable way, being risked. But it is also, sometimes, the person who praises, who promotes an interstice as a route to salvation. Thus we are sometimes a bit astonished by the extent of the interest generated by GNU, the General Public Licence, the invention of software users that authorises any and everyone to use and to modify a program under this licence, but which defines every program derived from it as falling under the same licence. It is opening a very innovative interstice endowed with the means to propagate itself thanks to the successful misappropriation of the usual role of property rights. But to go from that to seeing in it the forerunner of what will finally have the scalp of capitalism ... It would be wiser, in a more Chinese way, to celebrate this event in a way that gives others ideas and not – above all – in a prophetic way.

The desperate search for those who will take the place of the working class, those to whom the task of saving the world will fall, is the surest way of crushing interstices. If, one day, a social movement became capable of campaigning publicly by saying 'we don't want this medicine x', that is to say, of bothering pharmaceutical laboratories and the state at the same time, it would be necessary to affirm that it is a matter of a local event, and not a sign that announces a great change. Interstices need to be protected against the posturing of a hope that lends them a role in search of an actor, and constitutes them as the hostages of this role.

18
Ecosophy

In 1989, in his *Three Ecologies*, addressed to those who were engaged in the creation of a political ecology, Félix Guattari spoke of the necessity of an 'ecosophy', a wisdom of the milieu, one might say, or of what we have just called a 'thinking by the middle'. A fine term, milieu, one which (for once) gives French the advantage over English, since it designates at the same time the stake that a milieu constitutes for every living being, and the stake for thought of escaping from the hold of first or final reasons, those that arm a majoritarian position. Because whoever has such reasons can give no other role to others than that of having to be enlightened, convinced, mobilised.

Whoever thinks by the middle evidently doesn't submit to her milieu, but she is nevertheless situated in an experimental relationship to it, that is to say, at once both pragmatic and speculative. This is not a renunciation, at all, except for what concerns the powers that conjugate the double feeling of truth and duty, and that all converge on the denunciation of compromises and oppose theory to the entrapment by seductive appearances. We are not thinking theory against theory, because every theory transcends what matters to whoever thinks 'by the middle'. At whatever scale it may be, what matters in the first place will always be what no theory as such is able to provide, that is, the 'reconquest of a degree of creative autonomy in one particular domain'.[1]

How can the reconquest of a degree of creative autonomy be characterised so that it is not confused with the classic figure of a liberation or becoming conscious of, in which 'reconquest' is then in danger of being reduced to 'taking back what has been stolen'? How is one to escape the unavoidable dilemmas where what is in play is always presented in terms of judgements as to the 'true causes', as to what should be the only object worth reconquering, whatever its consequences may be?

How is reconquest to be defined in a way that is not poisoned by the 'progressive' ratification of statist–capitalist destructions? Capitalism is a source of alienation, OK, but at least it is one that has destroyed all the other forms of alienation and thus creates the conditions of possibility for a general emancipation ... In short, how is one to escape from what gives the very singular 'system of sorcery' with which we are dealing its hold? A 'system of sorcery without sorcerers' that is inseparable from a world where sorcery is not a matter of thought, being nothing but superstition?

Unhappily, today we cannot avoid the conclusion that the destruction or humiliating of attachments does not give birth to the free and responsible individuals that theory dreamed of. Neither here nor elsewhere. So, we think that ecosophy, the wisdom of the milieus, implies in the first place taking note of the devastated character of these milieus. That is to say, it implies the need to avoid like the plague every putting into perspective that would identify 'ecological disaster' with a tabula rasa that frees the way for 'reconquest'.

This does not signify that it is necessary to take the converse position, passing from disqualification to identification with a wisdom that we have lost or destroyed. We are accustomed enough to that, oscillating between triumphalism and guilt, between arrogance and the cult of what that arrogance has destroyed; and to the usual disappointment that results from the idea that it is enough to give the kiss of peace to what we wrongly defined as a hostile monster, turning the enemy into a friend.[2] That would still be to think of ourselves as being the only true actors, capable of making and of unmaking. In order to escape from the hold of this dream of grandeur, we will say that in the first place, to reconquer supposes an apprenticeship implying a certain humility: to learn to renew one's links with ancient practices that capitalism has dishonoured and which we have triumphantly believed we can do without. Practices that spoke of prudence in a fearsome world, of the possibility of creation despite the permanent probability of war.

For instance a word like 'commerce' should be thought anew, because it is one of those words that has been catastrophically emptied of its meaning and associated with the hold of capitalism. In all the poor countries where capitalism has become established, it works to destroy commerce and establish 'distribution networks'. But, the question 'is there a means of having commerce here, with these people?' is without doubt one of the oldest human questions, and the true art of commerce is the art of negotiation. It is an art that extends well beyond the domain of commodities and is much more demanding than the 'civilised commerce' praised by thinkers of the eighteenth century as synonymous with relations between humans that are finally pacified. In many traditions, to look after sick people is to know how to negotiate with invisible powers, how to have *commerce* with them. It is to learn what these powers, who have become enemies, want in compensation. Healers who know how to negotiate with invisible beings do not believe in the 'kiss of peace', they have no faith in the intrinsic goodwill of those they negotiate or haggle with. But one has to have participated in 'haggling' in countries where this art is still cultivated to know how the same word can designate indissociably both the exchange of goods and that of ideas, the 'commerce of minds', as one used to say.

To have commerce with is to calculate, it will be said, whereas it is precisely a matter of escaping from calculation. Let us be wary of this last formula, because what escapes from calculation can easily be identified with the incalculable, and the incalculable can be a figure of the transcendence to which one submits ... whatever the consequences may be. What matters from the pragmatic point of view is the mode of calculation. In the art of commerce there is a sort of technique of conjuring, an artifice that obliges one to slow down, to open the space in which the question of the mode of calculation can be posed. This is a detour that makes it possible to avoid defining exchange by the inert evidence of psychology, or by a 'market value', the transcendent role of which is to assign predetermined places to those who exchange.

We might say that in the two cases, commerce of goods and commerce of ideas, it is the slippery slope of what economists call the 'minimisation of the transaction cost' that must be warded off. The art of commerce is 'costly' in both time and patience. But it is what makes traders exist as obliged by a relation whose existence depends on them, as operating the co-production both of themselves in relation and of what links them together.

Hermes, like many other gods, was the god of traders, of writing and of thieves, the god of the ruse – *trickster* – and of exchange. An impure god, not really to be commended. Which is only natural. Whoever enters into a relation can be fooled, betrayed; every trader knows that he must pay attention to his own interests, never let himself get carried away by fusional enthusiasm, never 'have confidence in'. And yet, as with all pragmatics, commerce supposes a 'trust'. Not in the other but in the possible relation. In the fact that war, pillage, enslavement do not define the only 'realistic' horizon. *Calculemus*! said Leibniz, a mathematician-philosopher, but also a diplomat.[3] It was not at all a matter of an injunction to have to submit to a general model, but of the production of two inseparable processes: that which creates the 'consistency' of the problem, the dimensions that it makes hold together and which are required so that it might produce its own possibilities for a solution, and that which creates the 'us' of the problematic situation, of those who accept that this situation will find no other response than that of which they will become capable together.

Calculemus is perfectly suited to the new reference that has appeared in recent years marked by the new capitalist strategies founded on patent law, on the appropriation of what had to that point been defined, formally at least, as common goods. The reference is to the history of *enclosures* in England, of the *commons* around which the life of peasant communities was organised. Every Marxist knows that this new definition of the 'right to private property', became a synonym for the right to abuse, depriving peasants of what they depended on and turning them into the poor, in need of help, or driving them into the cities where they would give industry the primary material for limitless exploitation (the famous phase of the 'primitive accumulation' of capital). The novelty – which is illustrated perfectly by the movement organised around GNU in software – is the appearance of movements of 'users' resisting the abusive character of appropriation, one or another kind of appropriation, without being engaged in a general struggle for the abolition of the right to private property as such.

The notion of *users*, which is thus hardly prophetic, responds to the notion of *abuse*, which is always local, although now it proliferates everywhere. Of course, it is difficult to proclaim 'users of the world unite!' Each movement is particular and is thus exposed to the accusation of 'particularism', that is to say, to the type of mistrust generated among radical thinkers by movements 'betraying' the necessary universality of mobilisation. The thinkers of mobilisation are not wrong: these movements, which haven't stopped existing and recreating themselves in a variety of guises and with new objectives, don't offer any guarantee. Left to themselves, isolated, considered with suspicion, they have every chance of disappearing or of being absorbed by logics of management.

But it is a matter of a practical problem. Whether it is the press, internet networks, cooperative groups, SELs (systems of local exchange), NGOs, patient associations financing research programmes, the most varied defence committees, no interstice has ever had an a priori guarantee of survival – they can all be eaten up by the state or by capitalism. But neither are any of them condemned in advance. All may be conceived as experiments, as apprenticeships. And all need what each can learn.

This also signifies that each one needs to recognise itself and to be recognised by others as that whose apprenticeship matters for everyone.

We think that there is a great deal to learn from user movements; because the user is defined by *use*, a very interesting term because it cannot be reduced to simple utilisation. An object is defined by its utility, whereas a thing can enter into multiple uses, and no user can as such claim to be in a defining position. Every use is, in fact, minoritarian. Self-help groups judiciously presented themselves as bringing together drug 'users' because they knew that drugs are things that exceed consumption-based, medical or psychosocial definitions. That is why they were able to bring together the most heterogeneous of protagonists: none could claim to possess privileged access to the truth about drug use, a truth able to situate all other versions. One must learn about the uses of drugs, about what it is that uses are articulated around, because drugs are something to which attention must be paid if they are not to become destructive powers.

Certainly the notion of users can easily be diverted and it already has been. As soon as one hears talk of 'the rights of users', as soon as one accepts as users protagonists who define themselves as 'clients' or stakeholders – those whose needs must be satisfied at any cost – the diversion has taken place. By definition, the client is supposed to be indifferent to the means through which his demands will be satisfied. And one can understand why those who today direct public services, privatised or not, are so pleased to have abandoned the *user* for the *client*; he who demands to be properly served, in whose name the regulations inherited from past struggles for solidarity can be dismantled. The model of the client and the service provider is even on the point of becoming the rule at the heart of businesses themselves: everyone must satisfy demands and demands to be satisfied. Let the just but cruel calculations of supply and demand and cost–benefit analysis reign everywhere.

We are not maintaining that, everywhere today, user movements, which try to think against the definitions that oppose users to one another constitute the great force of the future, the force which will occupy *the* role of motor in the anti-capitalist struggle. But these movements interest us much more than movements of citizens, because they do not originate in a fiction of the state. Rather, the first thing they do is to provide us with a memory of a past that was violently destroyed, one in which uses fabricated attachments. They also speak to us of the price that public sector workers and their unions have paid and are still paying for the statist definition of their role. The user then becomes an anonymous 'anybody', requested not to meddle with things that don't concern him, suspected of being manipulated by those who would aim to weaken the rights of workers. When the operation of dismantling really began, it is hard not to be astonished that users didn't meddle very much with what 'didn't concern' them.

But user movements can also bear witness to rather remarkable inventions; to trajectories of apprenticeship that are innovative enough to silence the grand proclamations according to which the pasts of peasant communities are definitively dead, modern man henceforth being atomised, incapable of thinking beyond his immediate interests. It seems that when users with potentially conflicting interests are brought together in such a way that it is not a matter of arbitrating, of permitting and forbidding, but of envisaging together what they all depend on in different ways, then they are capable of creating concretely the means of distinguishing between use and abuse. Ceasing to be 'anybodies', they become capable of creating the means of distinguishing between manners of doing and the right to do, and this because they think, not as citizens – one (wo)man, one voice – but starting from what attaches them and obliges them to enter into commerce with one another.

The *calculemus* of users are only interesting when described in the particularity of their successes. But the latter are susceptible of giving ideas, of helping to resist the 'we have tos' that are always founded on the hypothesis of individuals incapable of thinking by and with one another. And above all, they are capable of resisting the seductions of the guarantee. Users don't offer any guarantee. They can always become *stakeholders*.

And it is precisely for that reason – because one cannot have confidence in them, but because their eventual force has a vital need of practices of 'trusting' and of 'paying attention' – that users are a rather good figure for what Deleuze wrote of as the left's need that people think.

19
Political Creation

If 'people thinking' is a necessary condition, what the left needs, it is not a sufficient condition. To define it as such would be to become vulnerable to the trap of the rather feeble utopia of 'spontaneity': it would be enough to give up grand, mobilising, theories, to let loose the 'creativity' of minoritarian groups fabricating their own co-ordinates, experimenting with their own locality, their own 'thing' in order for what holds us, miraculously, to give way and collapse.

The question is not at all to criticise such groups but to separate their eventual success from the question that preoccupies us here, that which makes us sounders of the depths. We have linked the efficacy of the system of sorcery that we are dealing with to the destruction of politics. The idealisation of spontaneous creativity ratifies this destruction, notably by identifying politics with a power that it would be a matter of not taking. The political question is not in the slightest a question that we want to impose on every minoritarian group, in the manner of an imperative arming a judgement. On the other hand, we want to maintain that political struggle also designates a question of creation and not a sort of spontaneous emergence at the heart of a milieu that a 'cooperation of brains' would suffice to characterise. *One doesn't do politics without knowing it.*

One can't forget ecosophy here either. Because most often it is the feeling of urgency, of the necessity of an engagement that cannot be denounced as a simple production of ethico-aesthetic jouissance, that poisons groups that are trying to do politics. This is part of the efficacy of the system of sorcery that we are dealing with: it is peerless in dividing those who want to confront it, including each of us inside ourselves, judged by ourselves in the name of this urgency which we are never up to. It is not surprising that the temptation of a reading of history that confers on a particular group the privilege of a political position indissociable 'by rights' from its practical identity, returns incessantly.

For instance, in McKenzie Wark's *A Hacker Manifesto*,[1] *hackers* are attributed a practice and 'class interests' that situate them beyond the particular interests of the 'exploited', whose horizon would be limited to a collectivisation of property. The *hacker* is he (or she) who struggles for free information and who calls into question every form of appropriation, including that by producers of what they produce. This activates an ecosophical concern: the hacker of the *Manifesto* certainly constitutes a new and interesting protagonist (besides being defined as a quasi-terrorist by those who demand more and more repressive laws from the state against all forms of piracy). We fear only that the manner in which the hacker is defined still responds to the 'progressivist' form that evades the political question because it grants the right of some to define the interests of others as 'still particular' faced with a universal that has arrived at last. Politics begins when this form gives way to the question of practices that make the need that minoritarian groups have of one another exist.

In *A Thousand Plateaus* Deleuze and Guattari evoked an 'itinerant creation' implying an ambulant people of 'relayers'[2] in explicit contrast with a model society but perhaps also, implicitly, with absolute nomadism, hacker style. The model society is a majoritarian one – everyone has a place that is just or at least merited, but if hacker nomadism defines every model as a matter for détournement, it is vulnerable to the passion to disabuse as an end in itself. Itinerance and the passage of relays imply, for their part, the always relative fabrication of localities. Those who 'itinerate' are always somewhere, never 'no matter where', they are always engaged by this experimentation here and now on this terrain, never freely traversing a smooth space, where everything is the same. As for the relayers evoked by Deleuze and Guattari, they are certainly not submitted to a model or a norm of fidelity that would authorise the relay, but the practice of relays cannot for all that be confused with the right to take over and to put into circulation.

The passage of relays implies not only holding but also giving. For the relay to be taken, it must be given, even if those who give know that they are not masters of what they give, that when a relay is taken it is not a matter of a simple translation but of a new creation. In this regard Félix Guattari evoked a process of 'existential catalysis', wherein each 'creation' or reconquest is able to generate repercussions in the mode of the 'yes, it's possible', able to arouse the appetite that will make another possibility exist elsewhere.

The figures of itinerance, of the passage of the relay, of existential catalysis, have a common trait. They all have as condition that what is produced locally – locally, always locally (for whoever thinks by the middle, there is only ever the local) – is also the production of what Deleuze and Guattari called desire, and others have called 'joy'. Minoritarian productions can be laborious, sometimes painful, they nonetheless differ from the 'becoming conscious of' associated with the loss of illusions, the recognition of a truth that transcends what is consequently no longer anything but illusion. The experience of the difference in the making between submitting to and creating, between accepting in the mode of the anonymous 'we have to' and discovering/exploring/fabricating the degree of creative autonomy that can be reconquered, has nothing to do with the classical version of emancipation, which – as the release from alienation – constitutes an eminently general model, generalisable without re-creation. We will say that this experience is what happens whenever a situation has received what never belongs to it by rights, or never 'naturally': the power to oblige thought.

Curiously enough, if there is one practice that allows the link between 'creative autonomy' and 'obligation' to be glimpsed, it is that of scientists. More precisely that of scientists when – and to the extent that – the practice that engages them is not reducible to the respect for a method supposed to guarantee the production of objective knowledge. That is to say, when – and to the extent that – this practice implies the success of a 'getting a hold'. We have already seen that in the case of experimenters, this success may be called the production of a 'fact' whose interpretation will resist objections. One may say that in this case the 'successful fact' has acquired what, in general, facts don't have, that is to say the capacity to produce agreement between those who are interested in it. An obligation corresponds to this definition of success: an experimenter will be obliged to recognise every objection as legitimate and welcome, on condition that this objection is 'competent', coming from an objector obliged to think and to imagine by the same definition of success.

The competent objection is not supposed to pursue any other end than that of putting to the test the proposition it calls into question, it is supposed to disregard every other type of interest. That is why the development of experimental practices, which confer on the verification of the successful experiment the power to oblige thought, is historically inseparable from the development of communities of 'competent colleagues'. These communities laid claim to an autonomy that can be understood as protecting them against the imposition of other ends, as ensuring a space inside which an idea or proposition has no value for itself and all that matters is its eventual capacity to overcome colleagues' objections. In this case, then, creative autonomy signifies the creation of spaces that assemble the 'competent' united by a minoritarian obligation: it is the possibility of a particular, non-generalisable, kind of success that makes them think, imagine, object.

But the example of the scientists has another aspect, that of a political and ecosophical catastrophe. It offers us the occasion to underline the ambiguity of the term 'autonomy', the signification of which varies according to the manner in which whoever vindicates their autonomy defines as much what their milieu is as what they are. Scientists have not presented their successes as always selective and risky but as assured by a method, and what is more, a general method, one for every terrain, associated with the equally general values of objectivity and rationality. Majoritarian values that 'anyone' should accept. As a consequence they have favoured the confusion between what unites them and what one may call pseudosciences, which reduces what they are dealing with to that which can be methodically observed and quantified. And they have defended the autonomy that they needed by defining 'non-scientists', by way of contrast, as subjective and irrational, that is to say, by defining their milieu as what they should be protected from. The autonomy vindicated by scientists destines them, then, to having public authorities and industry as their only worthwhile interlocutors, not because they would be rational, but because they have the means of feeding scientific research in exchange for the 'golden eggs' it would produce.

This example is the exact antithesis of a practice of relayers. Relayers would have required an itinerant definition of what a success is, a definition that ought to reinvent itself whenever a situation changes – and it would have to each time it concerns new people and new interests. Further, relaying the scientific practice, connecting success and passing the test of objections would mean assembling not only 'competent' protagonists but accepting the test of new types of objectors, not sharing the same obligations. What the sciences have given to those who fed them is not only the possibility of new powers of doing [*faire*], but also, and perhaps above all, new powers of silencing [*faire taire*], of suppressing objections, in the name of an apolitical scientific rationality – ecopathology.[3]

Every minoritarian practice that only has majoritarian words for speaking its need for autonomy will be tempted to envisage its milieu in missionary, ecopathological terms: bringing to 'others' what they lack, even if it means allying with all the powers having an interest in defining those 'others' as weak and 'lacking'. And in that way it will have lost every possibility of protecting itself in a political way. This is the case today, when the powers that scientists trusted no longer keep their distance and undertake to directly enslave what they had hitherto profited from while respecting certain forms. Sadness and resentment: we are no longer respected, 'they' demand that our work be evaluated in terms of 'results', that our work pass through the filter of the interests that feed it. For instance, 'they' demand that it be constrained and channelled by the stakes of patents: either patents that already exist, and as such suffice to make a work unprofitable, or patents to be applied for, including those the prime interest of which is to make the work of others unprofitable.

There is no reason to rejoice over the contemporary processes of transformation of scientific practices, which demand that scientists bend like everyone else to the 'we have to' and engender new types of 'minions'. That would be to fall into a trap, always the same trap – that of rejoicing over a capitalist destruction as of an act of justice that hits all those who, in any case, were unworthy of being protected. On the other hand, it is important to propose another mode of dramatisation of what happens to them, one that refuses the nostalgia of a golden age when the state fed 'disinterested' research and combats the apocalyptic themes of the type 'rising tide of irrationality'.

And the same necessity of inventing is posed each time that the state dismantles that which, at other times, it had chosen to feed in the name of majoritarian values. Science, culture, social security cannot be defended in the name of a past when the state was supposed faithful to its mission. That is why, in all these cases, it has to be a matter of a political creation, of a 'reconquest', against the convergent, majoritarian values in the name of which what is attacked had first become the 'business of the state'.

Evidently enough, there is a radical dissymmetry between a majoritarian politics, which mobilises around consensual values (the defence of science, culture, social security and so on), and a process of political creation. Besides, it is not a matter of abandoning the one in the name of the other: there is no reason not to struggle against the redeployment of statist–capitalist strategies, against the process of redefining what the public authorities (at every level) allow capitalism to do and what capitalism makes the public authorities do. This kind of mobilisation responds to urgency, but we think that one loses nothing by abandoning every pedagogico-triumphalist reference of the kind: this time 'they' have gone too far, 'the people' will understand and ... ('X, you're screwed, the people are in the street'). Triumphalism may obliterate the need to think what the political process needs, that is to say, in the first place, its need for protection from what poisons it.

How is one to become capable of creation if this capacity is not a dormant right that the interested parties will be able to recuperate as soon as the injustices of which they are the victims are suppressed? That is to say, if this 'becoming capable' is of the order of the event? In the first place the event must be protected from the ideas of spontaneity and unpredictability. Seattle was an event, but it was in preparation for a long time. There is an art of the event. But the word 'art' is a little too reassuring: it generates feelings that are elevated, but which don't oblige thought. One might also speak of a 'poetics'. In the same way that 'art' communicates with trade, poetics retains a link with 'making', 'fabricating', 'poiesis'.

Thought as obliged is emphatically not thought as adherence. It demands 'friction'. In order to resist the possibilities of making adherence too immediate and easy, we will risk proposing that a *technical* question responds to the cry 'needing people to think'.

20
Empowerment

To use the word 'technique' is, of course, a provocation. Not for the fun of it, though, but because the negative conditioned reflexes that this word generates form part of the pitfalls that we wish to diagnose. There is a pitfall each time that the kind of history that has produced us finds itself linked with whatever might be of the order of the self-evident.

The pitfall that it is a matter of naming here is the feeling of scandalised contempt that is quite predictably generated by the idea that success or failure, where people 'becoming capable of thinking' is concerned, can communicate with a 'technical' question, not with a question of truth or authentic freedom. We are that habituated to opposing technique and truth, fabrication and authenticity, manipulation and autonomy! We will not say that these oppositions that poison us are produced by capitalism, but we think that they form part of what renders us vulnerable to its operations of capture, of what it has profited from and what it presupposes. That things are defined as manipulable and humans take themselves for free, autonomous subjects: this is exactly what it requires.

It is a matter then of affirming that the self-evident fact according to which technique is by definition an instrument of domination, the negation of human freedom, is the product of our history, marked as it is by a rather extraordinary discrepancy. Since capitalism undertook to 'liberate productive forces', so-called 'material' techniques haven't stopped making new possibilities exist, inventing the means of making electrons, bacteria, viruses, and many other beings that humans didn't have the slightest idea of two centuries ago, do the most remarkable things ... And these means don't have very much to do with domination but much more with learning what it is that such beings may become capable of.

On the other hand, the only 'human techniques' that have progressed are the well-known ones that favour the contrary of thought, adherence (that of consumers, of workers, voters, militants and so on). It is enough to refer to what is perpetrated in schools, to the pseudo-science of pedagogy, and to the evaluation of knowledge as 'competence', to conclude that we haven't learned very much about what renders one capable of learning – quite the contrary, in fact. But also to think that this is not a coincidence. According to Michel Foucault, the school is no more made for learning from its failures than prison is. But it is peerless in producing adherence to the selection that it operates: everyone has their chance, and those who fail deserve to.

Everyone who has participated in meetings supposed to gather together 'free' beings knows that democratic goodwill, the 'everyone has the right to speak', 'everyone will get their turn', 'no, you may not speak now, others asked first', are not the best way to respond to the need for people to think. If – even in groups united by the minoritarian choice of not submitting – the voices of silence could be amplified, one would hear the sad seething of resentment, powerlessness, self-hate: 'I'm not going to complicate the situation further'; 'they all agree'; 'people will say I'm a traitor'; 'it's always the same who speak'; 'in any case, I have nothing to propose'; 'they know better'; 'people will say I'm frightened'; 'if no one is saying it, it's because it's idiotic'; 'since no one is interested in what I am saying, I'll keep quiet'.

Most of those who are reading us have experienced the manner in which an initial exaltation can thus surreptitiously turn into a taking of hostages, despite the best will in the world. All those who keep their doubts quiet in order not to betray the homogeneity of the group will be hostages. To the point of brutal rupture in some testing situation, when each is confronted, alone, with the dreadful choice: shamefully giving up or joining those who demand that the struggle continue till the heroic defeat.

And there is worse. We are thinking of the manner in which so many effective struggles terminate, when those who suggest making do with what has been gained are the target of excommunications that are not only humourless but mobilize what might be called an unequalled hatred. A nasty joy [*joie mauvaise*], as if finally one was dealing with the Enemy. Here, at last, all those traitors who – when their backs were against the wall – refused the struggle to the bitter end and showed their true face, are unmasked. Here is the moment of truth that will allow the 'pure' to recognise each other and separate themselves from everyone else: only a few will remain but the Cause will have won because all of those who would, in any case, have betrayed it have been unmasked and identified. Moreover those who have been stigmatised as traitors will often confirm this judgement: they will often become minions, for instance, loyal and forgetful artisans transforming the resources they eventually obtained into a new source of infernal alternatives. But do all of those who 'sell out' in this way reveal their 'true nature'? When the operation of purifying judgement takes over a situation, takes it hostage, doesn't it doom those who are rejected to join the enemy with whom they have already been identified?

All that is the 'natural' tendency. And our hypothesis is that to thwart this tendency demands not the ideals of a goodwill – which are likely to increase the taking of hostages – but the production of techniques, artifices, which actively take into account what is to be avoided. Activists who have chosen the strategy of non-violent confrontation have been inventors of such techniques, because their choice made their own vulnerability to this natural tendency crucial. In effect, they had to learn how to resist the test that every non-violent action implies: not to give way to what is, and remains, a temptation – how not to hit the cop who is hitting one of your friends! – and this in a situation in which the adversary will do everything in his power to encourage the temptation. They have had to ask themselves how, in the very process of decision about an action, they can make a force exist that holds the action together, although each member of the group individually will be confronted with the temptation. What has been learned is the danger of all procedures of collective decision-making (including, incidentally, those of the collective that each of us are) that risk silencing some, taking them hostage or profiting from that silence.

'Consensus' modes of decision-making are very fashionable today. But it is forgotten a little too often that the stake of consensus, such as it is experimented with by the practitioners of non-violent action, is not limited to avoiding a decision of the majority against minority, to refusing the verdict 'you have expressed your thoughts, we have voted, you have been beaten, you must bow to the decision if you are a "democrat"'. If consensus simply becomes a new imperative defining what must be attained, it may be productive of terrorising effects that are even more intense than the majority decision.

Techniques of *empowerment*[1] experimented with by non-violent activists[2] have as their vocation precisely the successful avoidance of inextricable mixtures of terror and loyalty that such an imperative is able to generate. They have as their aim that of rendering those who participate in a collective capable of thinking, of taking a position, of creating together that which none of them would have been capable of by themselves.

It is indeed a matter of techniques, of the perfecting of artifices and procedures. Constraints and roles have been created and experimented with pragmatically. Those who assume a role, notably in a process of deliberation, have as their task the complication of the process of taking a decision, and the role signifies that their interventions must escape all psychological or intentional interpretation.

Thus the responsibility of the person who has the role of the 'snake' is to signal the silence of some or the fact that others have objected but haven't been listened to and have been quiet since. The snake is not, for all that, a righter of wrongs, a defender of the weak. She does not denounce those who speak, she obliges them to slow down. Correlatively, it is not a matter of understanding what those who haven't been listened to 'wanted to say', or what those who didn't speak kept quiet about, nor of interpreting their attitude in a psychological way. The role of the snake affirms the undecidability of reasons, the deliberate refusal to pose the question of knowing if the concern, the silence, the timid and quickly stifled objection designate persons as persons or if they are to be connected with interesting aspects of the situation itself that are being expressed through them. What the persons may well have lived in a psychological mode (no one is listening to me, so I'm going to sulk) is transformed into an ingredient that is necessary to a process that has nothing psychological about it.

Here, artificially created undecidability is the condition for the event: becoming – in the strong sense of this word – everybody's concern, the heterogeneity that complicates the process of decision-making can be understood as testifying to the heterogeneity of the situation itself.

Such an event can be formulated thus: the situation that 'needs people to think' and that has to render them capable of thinking, has effectively received the force to make them think. Those who are united around a decision to take or a question to resolve no longer show respect for each other 'as humans'. But they do know and feel that if the manner in which they envisage the situation profits from the silence of some, it is the creation of the problem that this situation proposes that will have been mutilated. It is not, then, a matter of a moral rule, translating an idea to which everyone ought to submit, but of a pragmatic rule, whose value stems from what it makes exist. The role of the snake has no meaning independently of the transformation that it induces: a process which asks its protagonists not to express themselves but to become capable of being obliged to think by the situation and for the situation.

But *empowerment* is not in the slightest bit restricted to decision-making processes. How people have bitched, expounded and sniggered about the womens' groups in the 1970s who learned that it was sometimes necessary for them to meet together 'without men'! They were called 'witches', and it was an insult, but in fact in their groups they accomplished the first gesture of witches, without first naming it as such: the casting of the circle, the creation of the protective space necessary to the practice of that which exposes, of what puts at risk in order to transform. In these groups, indefatigably, everyone listened to each other tell a personal story, which had to that point been a secret, intimate treasure of her private suffering. And it was not a matter of denunciation, since they were among friends, but of assisting, in the strong sense of this word,[3] in the coming into existence of a new version of what had happened to them all. It was a matter of participating in an event for which thought, the 'becoming capable of thinking together', that which everyone had thought unique, shameful, inadmissible, was the stake.

Not, we must insist, a theoretical stake or one that is reflexive in the sense that reflexivity translates a keeping at a distance. But certainly one that is reflexive in the sense of a sound that is reflected from vibrating body to vibrating body, where one no longer needs to know who is the source of the sound and who echoes it in another mode, with other tonalities. Not the triumph of the same, in the sense that this same would designate a well-defined object, the matter of a theory, but the creation of a question that transforms. These women's groups are associated with what is sometimes understood as a slogan: 'the personal is the political'. As an all-purpose [*tout-terrain*] slogan it is rather terrifying, like every all-purpose judgement. Inside the circle of women, it was a matter of a becoming, of a recreating of the power of thinking and acting where previously only victims had existed.

We can now be more precise and, beginning from these two examples, distinguish what opposes the techniques of *empowerment* and the usual psychosocial techniques, which generate adherence. The latter (falsely) resemble so-called material techniques, because they pretend to be valid for all, that is to say, they would owe their efficacy to a definition of the human that looks scientific, because this definition refers to explanations that transcend the situation. As a result however, the human is always explained in terms of submission, of weakness. This is the curse of current ideas about science, in that the more a description characterises us as submissive (to our genes, our neuronal circuits, our ideologies, our systems of domination, our position in the social field, our unconscious, our cultural beliefs and so on), the more it seems 'scientific'. By contrast, a technique of *empowerment* does not present itself as deriving from a theory that would legitimate it. It is experimented with, and is only valid to the extent that it is efficacious, that it makes possible what it nevertheless cannot explain: the event of a becoming capable of thinking and feeling in a mode that escapes from the generalities that ask for adherence.

That is why the slightly contemptuous qualification that is sometimes reserved for so-called 'pre-scientific' or 'non-scientific' techniques, of 'recipes', is suitable for these techniques. In effect, what recipes are usually reproached with is that they do not have the power of explaining why they 'work' in terms that transcend the situation in which they 'work'. They do not have the power to describe the situation in a mode that is immediately generalisable to other situations. In other words, recipes are always 'minoritarian'. But that is precisely why they are a matter of relay (or of stealing): they cannot be borrowed without also being taken up again differently, reinvented, modified, or if one tries another recipe, interrogated so as to learn what it is a good idea to pay attention to.

We therefore have to reformulate our statement. Political creation, the people of relayers, calls for a culture of recipes, which aren't assimilable to theories. Recipes, which could very well also be what a group that experiments ought to make itself able to recount, in a pragmatic mode. This would mean being interested as much by their successes as their failures in order that they catalyse imaginations and fabricate an experience for 'the milieu', which avoids the need for each new group to have to 'reinvent everything' from scratch.

Make no mistake: whoever says recipe is not saying a feeble, second-order technique. If the recipes of *empowerment* do not refer to a theory that would justify them, it is because the question of justification is a poor question in relation to what their success designates, the event of a becoming. Such recipes do not explain, and do not aim at assuring the reproduction of what it is a matter of succeeding in doing, in the manner of an experimental protocol, any more than they aim at defining this success by conditions that would make it reproducible. An event is not reproducible, but it is possible to explore the possibilities of bringing about its repetition, which is risky and different every time.

A form of 'giving thanks', which protects the event from its transformation into a right, is appropriate for such a repetition. And 'protecting' techniques of *empowerment* is all the more necessary as the term has in fact already been dishonoured. One talks today of *empowerment* when it is a matter of ordering the 'weak' to 'motivate themselves', to 'responsibilise' themselves, to 'get active', to accept that there are no rights without responsibilities. And it is also spoken of when it is a matter of destroying a little bit more of what was politically constructed, that is to say, when it is a matter of undoing the 'heavy, conservative' procedures that get in the way of the possibility that the 'real actors' of a situation best profit from the opportunities that it offers them. Let the thousand flowers of transformation decided by those they concern bloom! Let the 'interested parties', the *stakeholders*, 'empowered' at last, liberated from the constraints of state and administration unite! Let them agree in a way that is best for their respective interests, let them mobilise for the good of the business, the school, the university, the hospital, the neighbourhood and so on. The market will judge.

To nevertheless risk defending this word *empowerment* is to take a stand against sorcery instead of undergoing its effects of capture, instead of deploring the misappropriation, or worse, of justifying it by diagnosing where *empowerment* was effectively vulnerable to capture. But to do that, it is necessary to employ words that resist the hold, which cannot be uttered by an executive of the WTO or a CEO with impunity.

The word 'magic' is one of those words. As the neo-pagan witch Starhawk writes,[4] to utter the word 'magic' is already an act of magic: the word puts to the test, compromises, exposes to sniggering. It forces us to feel what it is in us that balks and which is, perhaps, precisely what renders us vulnerable to capture. That is why we have decided to expose our readers to a last test, and in the process expose ourselves too: to try to take seriously those Americans who have dubbed themselves 'neo-pagan witches' and have cultivated the heritage of techniques of non-violent action in a mode that combines 'resisting capture' and 'learning to give thanks'.

21
Reclaim

If the singularity of capitalism is to be a 'system of sorcery without sorcerers', struggling against such a system imposes the need to make its procedures visible, sensible. And never to relinquish what it has captured, as if the operation of capture constituted a judgement of truth. It imposes the need never to say or even to think 'it was recuperated, therefore it was recuperable'.

And it will be said even less when it is a matter of our 'society', where the rule is now the control of commitment or motivation, and the endless self-mobilisation wherein workers must invest in their work body and soul or the unemployed must be ready to accept anything at all as work (because without work, they have to recognise, they are nothing but living dead). Because what is then 'recuperated' is well and truly that which the notion of 'labour power' only translated the purchase of for a determinate period of time: living labour itself, or even what was called the 'soul' in the time when one was still able to talk of 'stealers of souls'. It is no longer a matter of a pseudo-contract – that of your time at work against your salary – but of a capture 'body and soul'.

When an operation of capture succeeds, then, one will learn instead to yell, to cry, to find words that rise up like lamentations to speak this disgrace, to transform it into a force that obliges one to think/feel/act. It is because today's activist witches have learned this art (or *craft*) of transformation that they matter to us, that we are making ourselves their relay here.

One might say, in the manner of Deleuze about the right and the left, that between these witches and the sorcerous labouring of capitalist minions, there is much more a difference of nature than an opposition. Opposition is perfectly compatible with a certain homogeneity. For example, that of a submission, when people who oppose capitalism submit to the unavoidable dilemmas that become established when we reason as if we were the brain of humanity. The art of witches is that of a resistance to this submission, a resistance to the 'we have tos' that minions make into a principle of legitimacy. The way Starhawk's texts, posted on the web since Seattle, have been translated into French by many in a spontaneous manner, just feeling the need to relay them, testifies to this art.[1] As if they possessed the virtue of existential catalysis that Guattari spoke of. As if they made people think and feel in a way that one then wishes to propagate because one has experienced their efficacy, that of an antidote to the dilemmas poisoning the possibility born in Seattle.

The witches learned this art in the moment of greatest distress, during the election of Ronald Reagan in 1980. It is then that the mutation of a tradition, the Wicca tradition[2] (re-)born in England and exported to California, was produced. It then became a field for experimentation, cultivating the art of rituals able to give the inheritors of feminist, non-violent, anti-imperialist, ecological struggles the strength to resist the ordeal. The recipes of the witches were thus reinvented in a political mode, whilst conserving their capacity to appeal explicitly to what does not stem from goodwill but from the event that makes people capable of thinking and feeling. Whilst a system of sorcery can function without sorcerers who recognise themselves as such, those who have made the choice of calling themselves witches and activists have posed the hypothesis that to resist such a system, to learn to struggle against it, imposed the rediscovery/reinvention of old resources, the destruction of which has probably contributed to our vulnerability.

To call oneselves 'witches' is a part of this apprenticeship. From this point of view, the experience of activists who mobilised to defend native Indian populations that were under threat and who found themselves being asked 'it is kind of you to come and help us, but who are you, where do you come from?' was important. This was a question that those whose (feminist, non-violent, anti-imperialist) struggle only had all-purpose words for the denunciation of injustice and oppression could not answer. Because these words nullified the other who posed the question: 'for me, you are no matter who, it is the injustice and oppression of which you are the victims that brings me here'. But it was also a terrible question for those who had come in search of the spiritual wisdom of the Indians, a route to salvation through conversion.

To call oneself a 'witch' then was to learn to present oneself in a mode that catalyses the memory of the last great eradication not to concern colonised peoples but which happened at the very place in which capitalism was invented. It was to *reclaim* the heritage of the defeated, of those who our pacifying, psychologising compassion – the unfortunate, harmless old victims of superstition – still routinely dishonours today. To affirm that one was neo-pagan was to recall (pagan first of all signifies peasant) that it was peasant communities, as well as witches, that were destroyed, those whose existence depended on the *commons* of which they were expropriated.

The words invented by present-day witches do not so much proclaim legitimate demands, the right struggles, inalienable rights, as make exist the wrenching split of the world, its pain and the little, obstinate forces which, like the weeds growing in the slightest interstice, are alone capable of pushing through cement and cracking the concrete.[3] And to make themselves capable of such words, they needed to learn to think themselves, following the feminists, in a mode that might speak this split and that might also speak the joy of a power that rises and returns, which no one owns, because it cannot be appropriated, only 'reconquered'.

It is perhaps the word *reclaim* that Guattari was missing when he spoke of 'reconquest'. Far from the sense of *reconquista* as a crusade against the forces of evil, this word associates irreducibly to cure and to reappropriate, to learn again and to struggle. Not to say 'it is ours' (compare the sad slogan 'everything is ours, nothing is theirs'), not to think ourselves victims, but to become capable once again of inhabiting the devastated zones of experience.

We are not witches and we are not able to make ourselves the relay of the goddess that the rituals of the witches appeal to. On the other hand, we want to attempt to learn starting from the test that they offer us. And more particularly, starting from the unavoidable dilemma that we might be tempted to oppose to them. Because we 'no longer' believe in supernatural forces, and above all we do not want to adhere to a 'faith that can save'. Will capitalism not have won if one has to conclude that in order to resist its hold one has to fabricate a religion for oneself? That we have to submit ourselves deliberately to practices whose aim would be to close our eyes that are at last open, our 'sober senses'?

If neo-pagan witches could be identified with a 'true', authentic tradition, the manner of their resistance could be respected, because we have the habit of tolerating the survival of traditions, indeed even of respecting the wisdom immanent to them. The test stems from the experimental, 'fabricated' character of their rituals and the undecidability that they confront us with. If one could say that they 'believe' in their goddess, that their rituals express a belief, the question would again be resolved, in the sense that we could put ourselves at a comfortable distance from them, explaining what they do by beliefs that we do not share. But what they present us with does not allow itself to be identified as a belief.

If one said to them 'but your goddess is only a fiction', they would doubtless smile and would ask us if we are among those who believe that fiction is powerless, or that behind every fiction there is something that should be explained in acceptable, scientific, rational or intellectually reliable terms. In terms that reassure. And straightaway this demand to be reassured puts us on the side of the believers, those who believe that they can classify, that they can separate out the 'true' causes from those that would only be superstition or would refer only to psychological, sociological, even psychoanalytical causes, causes that always explain weakness, never becoming.

What makes people uncomfortable, what is difficult to accept is that witches are pragmatic, radically pragmatic: truly experimental technicians, experimenting with effects and consequences. We have the habit of looking 'behind' the technique for what would justify it or provide a guarantee ... but a guarantee against what?

That is where all the reasons for our being uncomfortable, tempted to ask for something more, can rush in. These reasons, from generalities concerning human credulity to catastrophic historical precedents (the Nazis, sects and so on) are respectable, but they can also be poisons. And they are poisons as soon as they are produced so as to protect people other than those who object and who, most often, consider themselves as self-sufficient, having no need for such suspect nonsense. So as to protect people who are judged to be 'weak', since for their part they need the prosthesis of such nonsense.

And it is in reference to these 'others', defined by their vulnerability that those who object and ask for guarantees will protest: 'but it would be to open the door to ...' And will not be able to accept that a pragmatic proposition has no beyond, has no other response to their objections than what every recipe, whatever it may be, calls for: the necessity of 'paying attention'.

Neo-pagan witches have learned that in the first place the technique or the art, the *craft* that they call magic is not what has to be rediscovered, in the sense of an authentic secret. It is a matter of *reclaiming*, of reactivating. And it is also a matter of relaying the old knowledge that such an art forces one to pay attention, to protect oneself, that is to say in the first place and above all, not to think of oneself as sufficient unto oneself. They have learned (again) the necessity of casting the circle, of creating the closed space where the forces they have a vital need for can be convoked.

These forces are what 'users' will certainly need, if they are to resist the temptation to confuse use and utilisation. Which nomadic *hackers* will perhaps need when they think taking [*la prise*] against appropriation, but forget that 'to take' implies 'to receive'.

These are also the forces that associations of anonymous alcoholics, who have discovered that anyone who thinks they can get free from alcohol alone by their own willpower will always be beaten, know they need. Combat against alcohol begins not with the recognition of one's own weakness, which the order-word 'be strong' refers to, but by the recognition of the impossibility of getting free alone, because one is dealing with a power that is all the more fearsome as one tries to escape from it, a power which one must learn to address. 'Once an alcoholic, always an alcoholic' is the affirmation required so as to enter into different relations with alcohol.

Maybe every political creation needs those who it brings together to know how to make exist the fact that they need help in order for the situation to oblige them to think/feel. The circle of the pragmatics of witchcraft is a response to this need. It makes a situation exist that is irreducible to the 'free expression' of individual opinions.

To cast the circle is to fabricate a closure, a separation, the space of an experience that is irreducible to individual psychology, and which much rather puts in question those who call themselves individuals: all those who are brought together – big-mouthed or anxious, paranoid or plaintive, shit stirrers or thirsty for understanding – are in the first place all 'infected' or 'poisoned' equally, although in different modes, and all equally need what none among them is able to produce alone.

However, unlike anonymous alcoholics, the circle here does not have as its vocation to learn another mode of relation with what has captured you, in order that you may recover a 'normal' life outside the circle. Unlike scientists, it is not defined against a world that it would later conquer and convert. Unlike that of feminists and of non-violent protesters, it doesn't include human protagonists only. What is invoked there, she who, the witches say, 'returns' is she to whom thanks will be given for the event that makes each and all together capable of opening up and of learning. She who makes them capable, when opening the circle and parting, of encountering differently what it was first necessary to keep outside. To honour the goddess is to learn at one and the same time to close and to make exist, inside, the 'cry' of a world that demands that one learn how to join it again.

Open the circle, they say, so as to 'do the work of the goddess', work that the goddess does not dictate to them, the meaning of which is produced each time, here and now: not in the name of a theory, of abstract order-words, but with the freedom of opportunism. A very fine word 'opportunism' since it designates the meaning, which is a force, of what is opportune, of what is suitable for each situation, the meaning of *this* 'concrete' situation, accompanied by the halo of what can become possible. A word destroyed by those who wish for it to be theory or principles that guide action and guarantee choices without having to produce the force to think them.

We, who aren't witches, can understand the manner in which they invoke this immanent goddess, who it is not a matter of believing but to whom all the powers of change are attributed: 'she changes everything she touches, and everything she touches changes'.[4] The efficacy of this refrain[5] is to attribute the power of changing to her, above all so as not to attribute it to oneself. To honour change as a creation, instead of making it something 'natural': you only have to talk, if you have something to say. And to resist judgement in order to become capable of discerning the passage taken by a change.

To 'do the work of the goddess' is at one and the same time to learn to seize the opportunities through which a change can pass and to learn to 'leave to the goddess' what belongs to no one. The goddess is not 'supernatural', she does not 'know better', she doesn't take the place of a theory and is not a reference in an argument. The efficacy proper to the recipes that invoke her and call for her presence is the capacity to resist the manners of speaking that attribute the crushing, desperate responsibility of conceiving an action that is equal to the demands of the situation to those who struggle.

It is not a matter of refusing – with stupid confidence – the lack of proportion between what one is capable of and the knowledge that 'everything would have to change' but of welcoming it precisely in its excessiveness [*demesure*]: to refuse that anyone might make it an argument, an arm, an instrument of mobilisation with a majoritarian, always majoritarian, vocation and brush aside precarious possibilities in the name of global urgency.

'Circles are woven, circles unravel', say the witches, signifying two things indissociably: no situation is decisive in itself, authorising judgement and verdict; and every situation can be deliberately, experimentally, collectively 'fabricated', or 'woven' in such a manner as to avoid linking its truth to a *modus moriendi*, to a manner of proving by death that one was well and truly elected. Every circle is the exploration of a *modus vivendi*, which permits the situation to be lived in such way that if it comes undone, those who will have participated in the weaving come out of it more alive, having learned and become capable of teaching others what they have learned, capable of participating in other circles, other weaving processes.

No relay has the power of defining the manner in which it will be taken up again, but it belongs to the 'ecosophical' wisdom of neo-pagan witches to carry on the relay by not appealing to anything other than that which the situation obliges. After the Genoa protest and the violence of repression Starhawk wrote against the temptation to make the anarchists of the Black Bloc responsible: 'I want to win this revolution. I don't think we have the ecological or social leeway to mount another one if this fails. And the odds of winning are so slim that we can't afford to be anything but smart, strategic, and tight with one another.'[6] Faced with urgency, we cannot allow ourselves anything other than to learn to think, against the temptation to let the feeling of urgency dominate us.

The witch's proposition doesn't ask for the conversion of those to whom it is addressed. When witches address others, they do nothing other, all told, than relay, echo the question that transformed them themselves – existential catalysis. They tell us their recipes and ask us: 'And you, where do you draw your capacity to hold up and to act from? How do you succeed in creating the protection that the poisoned milieu in which we all live necessitates? What protects you from the vulnerability that our common enemy hasn't stopped profiting from? What do you do? What have you learned?'

And it is because it wasn't a matter of conversion but of commerce – an exchange of 'good procedures' – that we have experienced, without any guilt but with perplexity and a certain fright, the poverty of our responses and the necessity of struggling against what poisons the spaces in which responses could be created. That is what has 'obliged' us to try to adopt the position of sounders of depths.

Above all, not to Conclude

In a comment about a first version of our text, Patloch posed the question which is that of every pragmatic essay: 'it would be useful to know *how far it works* or *where it breaks down*, because depending on the case, it closes down or opens up an awareness, a perception and the eventual interest of everyone in picking up what has been laid out here'.

It is a question that has accompanied us throughout the composition of this text, but that has not prevented us from taking risks that prudence would have advised us to avoid. To end with witches, for example, exposes us – and we know it – to the conclusion that that is the model that we are proposing, that that is where we are surreptitiously leading. Here what we are trying would break down and we would have to accept the resulting flat refusal.

Those for whom the text has 'worked' will have grasped that we have tried to do something else entirely. To make the pragmatic challenge – which runs counter to all theoretical guarantees – exist, we have felt the need to fabricate what constitutes a veritable test for our habits of thought. It was a matter of going right to the point where critical lucidity – to which we are as attached as anyone else – finds itself challenged to diverge from its triumphalist double, the critical spirit. And one cannot attain this point in the mode that philosophers generally call reflexive, reflecting on oneself, bringing critical light to where an obscure assurance still ruled. Because such a reflexive mode still makes of us the brains, that which confronts the ultimate dilemmas without ever interrogating itself about what feeds it, attributing to itself a force that it is a witness to but that it doesn't know how to honour.

Put this way, it sounds very mystical, although it is really very practical (like every mystic, in fact). What it is a matter of honouring is not in question here. That may also be the hope of those who died appealing to the future, that is to say, to *us*, on whom their dying for nothing or not depends. On the other hand – and this was what made our text difficult, to write and to read – the test designates the very idea that what nourishes us should be honoured, nourished but not defined as 'good for everyone'.

Our text is difficult because at each step it had to thwart the possibility that it works 'too easily'. The idea, for example, that all these stories about witchcraft and *empowerment* can indeed be 'psychologically' useful, but that they are only good for the others who need such help. For it to have a chance of working as it ought to work, it was necessary to take the risk that it break down.

Another difficulty is that we have not responded to any of the burning questions of the day and have not unfolded any grand perspective on the future. However, presenting ourselves as being part of the heritage of Seattle, we cannot ignore the hesitations and disarray that gnaw away at this heritage, from which the vultures, the specialists of *post mortem* analysis, are already drawing the unsurpassable lessons.

We have not given our 'opinion' on divisive topics such as the condemnation of the French law against the hijab at the European Social Forum in London in October 2004. Or the presence of Tariq Ramadan at this forum. That doesn't mean that we judge such divisive questions to be insignificant. But what matters for us is the difference to be made between a movement of opinion – opinion always has an opinion on everything – and a movement that knows how to pay attention to the difference between questions that are 'imposed' and those that it succeeds in (re)creating. To learn to defend ourselves against the imposition of ready-made problems, to resist mobilisations for or against, has been one of our leitmotifs.

'Let's pay attention' is the plea of sounders of the depths. And it is not only a matter of pleading that one listen to 'them' as if this was a role that was attributable to certain people in a specific mode. Certainly artifice – that of an intervention like ours or that which techniques of *empowerment* put in place – happens by the taking of roles. But these roles are just as much manners of making hold together, under tension, dimensions that belong to the experience of each. Sounders of the depths do not address others who would be unable to pay attention. They can only be understood to the extent that this 'knowing how to pay attention' belongs to everyone, although in our world it is most often related to private 'psychological' qualities, those qualities that are attributed in a privileged manner to women.

If we have called into question the notion of 'theory' so frequently, it is precisely to the extent that it corresponds to sparing ourselves the bother of 'paying attention', to a principle of a priori judgement that has the power of separating what must guide thinking and what can be rejected as anecdotal. In doing so, we have once more exposed ourselves, this time to the accusation of empiricist anti-intellectualism. However, there is nothing more demanding, intellectually, affectively and imaginatively, than the process of creating a problem, above all if this process is political, that is to say, collective.

Theory, *such as we call it into question*, is what allows oneself not to bother having to go through this process, or the apprenticeship that it demands and what it obliges one to. This shortcut is what permits mobilisation. And once again our attempt can break down, because a response is foreseeable: doesn't the political creation that we are calling for at all levels need peace? Are we not at war, struggling against something that is capable of destroying all the subtle and precarious assemblages that we have elaborated with the back of its hand? Isn't dreaming of peace in a time of war a dangerous utopia?

Those for whom what we have attempted has 'worked' will have sensed the trap. And if they have sensed it, this is to the extent that we have succeeded in creating a resonance with the experience they have undergone in all those situations where the reference to war has fabricated hostages, has devoured those it mobilised. And has ended up convincing them that there was nothing to be done, submitting them to 'we have to'.

We are speaking under the test of the present, of 2004, and without even speaking of the war in Iraq, or of the global war declared against terrorism. We have in effect been living in a war regime for more than a quarter of a century. A war that is all the more obscene given that it presents itself as a 'natural', permanent state of affairs, with no conceivable peace in view. Our obsession with the power of the 'we have to' would doubtless not have inhabited us in the epoch when capitalism could adorn itself in the charms of progress, when the alternatives that it was ceaselessly constructing could be described as the conditions for this progress.

To call these alternatives 'infernal', to oppose them with political creation is to be situated after the charm has been dispelled, at the moment that we are forced to confront the fact that the construction can continue with renewed energy without the support of progress. We will not say that capitalism is showing its true face – we don't think that it has a face – but we are constrained to break not only with every ambition of a 'pedagogical' type, but also with all those 'economies' of thought that progress permitted. If there is a future worthy of the name, it will not be summed up as the appropriation of the fruits of progress by those who are its real producers.

So, to link the hold of capitalism with the fabrication of minions, with those captured by a 'we have to' that has become an end in itself, as we have done, is to try to think capitalism not in its theoretical truth (unveiled at last) but in the present. It is not a matter of defining but of proposing a way of getting a hold. And the primary characteristic of this way of getting a hold is that it has a vital need of 'paying attention', which has to be cultivated even in a time of war (above all in a time of war). What we have proposed depends on this 'paying attention'. For instance, we know that 'to name the minions' can easily lead to a new mode of denunciation, rather than communicating with the question of the protection that is needed. And that to speak of *empowerment*, in an epoch in which this word serves as a banner for all the enterprises of dismantling that can be gathered under the sign of 'neo-liberalism', is to expose ourselves to the accusation of playing the adversary's game, of weakening the collective resistance that today is more indispensable than ever.

In other words, we really do need those who read us to 'think', because we have given the critical spirit an embarrassment of riches when it comes to choosing the rope with which to hang us. Unless it doesn't even bother, appalled that we can find nothing else to oppose to capitalism than a magic that makes the accusation of 'illusionism' quasi-tautological.

We needed to bet on this putting of ourselves into a position of vulnerability because we wanted to address ourselves to those who are reading us by appealing to their force. We did not want to connive with those who define themselves as strong but brandish the weakness of 'others' in the manner of an instrument of censorship and self-censorship. The great motto of pragmatism is 'to trust' without for all that having confidence, to trust in the sense that its verification is an event, and not a due.

And so, above all, not to conclude, because the conclusion belongs to those for whom this has succeeded, for whom this has worked, because the words that we have proposed have helped them to trust what they felt already.

Notes

Chapter 1 Inheriting from Seattle

1. 'Circuit Breakers' is another possible translation for 'Les empêcheurs de penser en rond' which is now run by Découverte in Paris.
2. The term 'manière' is used recurrently throughout this text. It is perhaps most comfortably translated as 'way'. The direct translation as 'manner' has been conserved wherever possible here, because it has a technical meaning for the authors (compare, for example, with Gilles Deleuze's comments on 'mannerism' and the syntax appropriate to events, in *The Fold: Leibniz and the Baroque* (London: Athlone, 1993)). [Translator's note]
3. Etienne Souriau, *L'Ombre de Dieu* (Paris: PUF, 1955), pp. 91–3. Souriau distinguishes four types of figure: Sages, Visionaries [les Inspirés], Sounders, Adventurers, between which he doesn't establish any hierarchy. It may happen that, depending on circumstances, a person may adopt distinct roles (the two of us have both been adventurers). What matters is not to confuse the roles and not to attempt to play all the roles at once.

Chapter 2 What Are We Dealing With?

1. The French expression 'mot d'ordre' can be translated as 'slogan'. The expression 'order-words' has been adopted because of its consonance with the translation of 'mot d'ordre' in Gilles Deleuze and Felix Guattari, *A Thousand Plateaus* (Minneapolis: Minnesota University Press, 1987), to whom the authors refer on a number of occasions throughout this book. [TN]
2. In the original French text, this paragraph referred to a paper written by Greenpeace, and aimed to counter the incredulity that speaking about capitalism might generate for some readers. The paragraph has been modified because, as Professor Stengers points out 'everyone has been talking about capitalism since the financial crisis' (personal communication). [TN]
3. Stéphane Courtois et al., *The Black Book of Communism: Crimes, Terror, Repression* (Cambridge, MA: Harvard University Press, 1999).
4. The calling into question of 'big concepts' by Bruno Latour began with *Science in Action* (Cambridge, MA: Harvard University Press, 1987) and hasn't stopped; getting richer in novel consequences since. See *We Have Never Been Modern* (Cambridge, MA: Harvard University Press, 1993), *The Politics of Nature* (Cambridge, MA: Harvard University Press, 2004), *Pandora's Hope: Essays on the Reality of Science Studies* (Cambridge, MA: Harvard University Press, 1999), *The Making of Law* (Cambridge: Polity, 2010).
5. Compare Isabelle Stengers and Olivier Ralet, *Drogues: Le défi hollondais* (Paris: Les Empêcheurs de penser en rond, 1991).

Chapter 3 Daring to be Pragmatic

1. We will go a little further on this point in the second part of this book (Chapter 8: 'Marx Again ...').
2. I have rendered the French expression 'faire attention' as 'to pay attention'. It is worth noting here that the French has a broader range of meaning than the English expression, in that it can also mean 'taking care of (oneself)' or 'to be cautious' about something [TN].
3. For that matter it is the same with the 'objective' properties of the beings that result from experimentation: they have no meaning outside of the relationship that they have with the apparatuses that allowed them to be formulated.
4. 'Be the evils what they may, the experiment is not yet played out. The United States are not yet made; they are not a finished fact to be categorically assessed' (John Dewey, 'Pragmatic America', quoted in Robert B. Westbrook, *John Dewey and American Democracy* (Ithaca: Cornell University Press, 1991), p. 552). We dedicate this quotation to all of those who, as we write this note, are being tested by doubt and despair.

Chapter 4 Infernal Alternatives

1. In the French nursery rhyme to which the authors are referring, as the rest of the crew are deciding how the cabin boy will be eaten, the latter climbs the mainsail and addresses the heavens. [TN]
2. See Bruno Latour, *The Pasteurisation of France* (Cambridge, MA: Harvard University Press, 1993), and *Science in Action* (Cambridge, MA: Harvard University Press, 1987).
3. Michel Callon (ed.), *The Laws of the Market* (Oxford: Blackwell, 1998).

Chapter 5 Minions

1. Jean-Marc Moutot's film (released January 2004) shows the role of auditors and the training of a young person in the trade admirably.
2. The (al)chemico-pragmatic definition of gold: it 'resists' all acids except aqua-fort.

Chapter 7 Leaving Safe Ground

1. See notably Bruno Latour, *Pandora's Hope. Essays on the Reality of Science Studies* (Cambridge, MA: Harvard University Press, 1999).
2. Among them we will mention Donna Haraway. Not only because her texts are inhabited by these themes but also so as to contribute to her resistance against the way in which they have been transformed into 'post' manifestos. See notably Donna Haraway, *Simians, Cyborgs, and Women: The Reinvention of Nature* (New York: Routledge, 1991). See also the work of Maria Puig de la Bellacasa, to whom this chapter is deeply indebted.

Chapter 8 Marx Again ...

1. Karl Marx and Friedrich Engels, *The Communist Manifesto* (Harmondsworth: Penguin, 1967), p. 223.
2. 'Devant les Luddites'. 'Before' here means 'in the presence of', 'in front of', not 'prior to'. See Isabelle Stengers, 'William James: An Ethics of Thought', in *Radical Philosophy*, 157 on 'thinking before'. [See, http://www.radicalphilosophy.com/default.asp?channel_id=2188&editorial_id=28470.]

Chapter 9 To Believe in Progress no Longer?

1. A concept explored by Philippe Zarifian in, for example, *A quoi sert le travail?* (Paris: La Dispute, 2003).
2. The verb 'responsabiliser' would usually be translated as 'to make someone aware of his or her responsibilities'. The ugly, neologistic translation as 'responsibilise' has been retained here for what, after all, is an ugly idea.
3. Karl Marx and Friedrich Engels, *The Communist Manifesto* (Harmondsworth: Penguin, 1967), p. 224.
4. Félix Guattari, *The Three Ecologies* (London: Athlone, 2005).
5. The term that the authors use 'aquabonisme' derives from the expression 'à quoi bon?' – 'what's the point?' or 'why bother?' The French singer Jacques Dutronc wrote a song called 'L'aquaboniste' that is better known in English-speaking countries in its performance by Jane Birkin and Serge Gainsbourg. [TN]

Chapter 10 Learning Fright

1. See notably Tobie Nathan, *L'influence qui guérit* (Paris: Odile Jacob, 1994) and *Nous ne sommes pas seuls au monde* (Paris: Les Empêcheurs de penser en rond, 2004).

Chapter 11 Thanks to Seattle?

1. See, for example, Gilles Deleuze, 'Plato, the Greeks', in *Essays Critical and Clinical* (London: Verso, 1998), p. 136.

Chapter 12 The Trajectory of an Apprenticeship

1. For more details on what follows, see Philippe Pignarre, *Comment sauver (vraiment) le Sécu* (Paris: La Découverte, 2004).

Chapter 13 Fostering New Connections

1. See Philippe Pignarre, *Le Grand Secret de l'industrie pharmaceutique* (Paris: La Découverte, 2003).
2. Sheldon Krimsky, *Science in the Private Interest* (Oxford: Rowman-Littlefield, 2003).
3. See Perline and Thierry Noisette, *La Bataille du logiciel libre. Dix clés pour comprendre* (Paris: La Découverte, 2004).

Chapter 14 Sorry, but we have to ...

1. Not unlike, say, the National Insurance system in the United Kingdom, employers in France are obliged to pay a portion of their employees' salaries into social security. [TN]

Chapter 15 Reactivating History

1. The expression that the authors use is 'droits acquis'. 'Entitlements' doesn't have quite the same set of connotations but both expressions have both a legal sense and the more vernacular sense of something to which one has a 'right'. 'Vested interests' was another possibility here, although its 'corporatist' connotations and historical connections with the industrial disputes of the 1970s in the UK does not, perhaps, capture the more general sense that 'entitlements' has, even if the French 'droits acquis' keeps somewhat more of a connection with the idea of 'rights we have struggled for'. [TN]
2. An English-language edition of which, *Prescrire International*, can be accessed at www.prescrire.org. [TN]
3. In Part IV we will talk of a 'trust' [*faire confiance*]. Unlike 'having confidence in' [*avoir confiance*], which communicates with 'relying on', the accent will be placed on the 'doing' [*faire*].
4. Gilles Deleuze, *Negotiations 1972–1990* (New York: Columbia University Press, 1995), pp. 126–8.

Chapter 16 A Cry

1. The *Diagnostic and Statistical Manual of Mental Disorders*, published by the American Psychiatric Association, is a real 'herbarium' of mental health disorders. Successive editions have pursued the ambition that every psychiatrist in the world, faced with the same patient, would make the same diagnosis.
2. Or 'foreigners in an irregular situation' or 'illegal immigrants'. The expression '*sans-papiers*' became something of a media expression in France after the occupation of several churches in Paris by immigrants in the 1990s. [TN]
3. Gilles Deleuze and Félix Guattari, *A Thousand Plateaus* (Minneapolis: Minnesota University Press, 1987), especially pp. 320–3.

Chapter 17 Interstices

1. See Isabelle Stengers and Olivier Ralet, *Drogues. Le défi hollandaise* (Paris: Les Empêcheurs de penser en rond, 1991).
2. We take the expression 'penser par le milieu' – and a little of the thinking about it – from Gilles Deleuze and Claire Parnet, *Dialogues* (London: Athlone, 1989).
3. See Ann Coppel, *Peut-on civiliser les drogues? De la guerre à la drogue à la réduction des risques* (Paris: La Découverte: 2002).

4. It is not insignificant to note that in 'modern' managerial jargon (including the French), *stakeholders*, the 'partners' of a business (employees, clients, suppliers) are the virtuous counterparts – they are never listened to enough – of the *shareholders*, who are always suspected of being blinded by their obsession with short-term profits. Another variant of the infernal alternative.
5. See 'Public Perceptions of Agricultural Biotechnologies in Europe', http://csec.lancs.ac.uk/pabe/docs.htm.

Chapter 18 Ecosophy

1. Félix Guattari, *The Three Ecologies* (London: Athlone, 2000), p. 69.
2. 'Le Prince crapaud' is the French title for the fairy tale given canonical written form by the Brothers Grimm as *Der Froschkönig oder der eiserne Heinrich* – The Frog Prince. But a 'crapaud' in French is a toad. [TN]
3. Compare Isabelle Stengers, *Cosmopolitiques VII: Pour en finir avec la tolérance* (Paris: La Découverte, 1997), ch. 9. [TN]

Chapter 19 Political Creation

1. McKenzie Wark, *A Hacker Manifesto* (Cambridge, MA: Harvard University Press, 2004).
2. Gilles Deleuze and Félix Guattari, *A Thousand Plateaus* (Minneapolis: Minnesota University Press, 1987), p. 377.
3. An example of the power to silence: the 'it's only a placebo effect', which lumps together all the medicines invented in other worlds.

Chapter 20 Empowerment

1. [*Empowerment* was left in English in the original. This footnote, which explains that decision has been retained.] This word *empowerment* is difficult to translate into French. The worst proposal was 'responsibilisation', which communicates directly with the 'free and responsible' choice to subscribe to a pension fund, to work seventy hours a week and so on. But that's not the only reason why we have chosen to leave the term in English. It is also to pay homage to those who have created, where theories of alienation pretended to provide the solution. It will be the same further on with the word *reclaim*: the absence of a suitable French word is doubled in the 'French-speaking' world by the (relative) absence of practices the cultivation of which affirms at the same time both the poisons that it is a matter of finding a cure for and the fact that goodwill is not enough.
2. Knowledge of these techniques is transmitted above all via the internet. Do not forget to add 'direct action' to 'empowerment' and to 'consensus' when using a search engine, so as not to be drowned in 'managerial' literature. See also Starhawk, *Dreaming the Dark: Magic, Sex and Politics* (Boston: Beacon Press, 1982) and Starhawk, *Truth or Dare: Encounters with Power, Authority and Mystery* (San Francisco: HarperSanFrancisco, 1988).
3. The verb 'assister' means 'to be present at', 'to witness' as well as 'to assist' and 'to aid'. 'Assister à une réunion' means 'to attend a meeting'. [TN]
4. Starhawk, *Dreaming the Dark*, pp. 24–5.

Chapter 21 Reclaim

1. Some of these texts have been collected in Starhawk, *Parcours d'une altermondialiste: De Seattle au Twin Towers* (Paris: Les Empêcheurs de penser en rond, 2003). All the texts were translated for free.
2. The Wicca movement rediscovered/revived/rehabilitated the witches demonised by their Christian persecutors. And it recreated their rituals addressed to an Earth Goddess, an immanent power called Artemis, Astarte, Athena, Melusine, Isis, Cerridwen, Brigid, Hecate, Lilith and many other names.
3. Starhawk, *Webs of Power* (Gabriola Island: New Society Publishers, 2002), p. 28.
4. Starhawk, *Dreaming the Dark: Magic, Sex and Politics* (Boston: Beacon Press, 1982), p. 81.
5. We borrow this word from Deleuze and Guattari, *A Thousand Plateaus* (Minneapolis: Minnesota University Press, 1987), where it names that which at the same time closes, creates an 'at home', and generates the movement of going out, 'launching forth'. The chapter 'Of the Refrain' distinguishes between romantic refrains, where it is a matter of joining with the forces of the earth, of the natal and the people, and 'cosmic' refrains which capture and make visible 'non-visible' forces that are irreducible to a mythic identity. And Deleuze and Guattari emphasise that this distinction is one of technique, 'exclusively one of technique' (p. 377). Perhaps one could say that the manner in which the Wicca tradition has been reinvented, transformed into an experimental technique of resistance to capitalism, testifies for its part to the making of a strange undecidability between earth and cosmos.
6. Starhawk, *Webs of Power* (Gabriola Island: New Society Publishers, 2002), p. 127.

Index*

*Index compiled by M. Beatrice Fazi.

GPSR Compliance
The European Union's (EU) General Product Safety Regulation (GPSR) is a set of rules that requires consumer products to be safe and our obligations to ensure this.

If you have any concerns about our products, you can contact us on

ProductSafety@springernature.com

In case Publisher is established outside the EU, the EU authorized representative is:

Springer Nature Customer Service Center GmbH
Europaplatz 3
69115 Heidelberg, Germany

www.ingramcontent.com/pod-product-compliance
Lightning Source LLC
Chambersburg PA
CBHW072011251225
37172CB00030B/281
9780230237629